AQA
Science
for GCSE
FOUNDATION

Revision guide

Ben Clyde

Series Editor:
Keith Hirst

From Harcourt

Heinemann Educational Publishers
Halley Court, Jordan Hill, Oxford OX2 8EJ
Part of Harcourt Education

Heinemann is the registered trademark of
Harcourt Education Limited

© Harcourt Education Limited 2007

First published 2007

11 10 09 08 07
10 9 8 7 6 5 4 3 2 1

British Library Cataloguing in Publication Data is available from
the British Library on request.

10-digit ISBN: 0 435675 52 4
13-digit ISBN: 978 0 435675 52 3

Designed by Ken Vail Graphic Design
Project managed, edited and typeset by Bookcraft Ltd
(Alex Sharpe, Project Manager; Helen Barham, Editor)

Harcourt project team: Marcus Bell, David Cooke,
Andrew Halcro-Johnston, Sarah Ross, Ruth Simms, Iti Singh

Original illustrations © Harcourt Education Limited 2007

Illustrated by Beehive Illustration (Martin Sanders, Mark Turner),
Bookcraft India Pvt Ltd (Gemma Raj), Nick Hawken, NB Illustration
(Ben Hasler, Ruth Thomlevold), Sylvie Poggio Artists Agency (Rory
Walker)

Printed in Italy by Printer Trento S.r.l.

Cover photo © Superstock

Every effort has been made to contact copyright holders of
material reproduced in this book. Any omissions will be rectified
in subsequent printings if notice is given to the publishers.

Contents

How to use this book   iv

Revision and exam advice   v

B1a   Human Biology

1   Body conditions and health   2   2   Drugs and disease   6

B1b   Evolution and Environment

3   Variation and evolution   10   4   Taking care of the planet   14

C1a   Products from Rocks

1   Earth provides   18   3   Oil: black gold   26

2   Useful metals   22

C1b   Oils, Earth and Atmosphere

4   Oil is not just for energy!   29   6   Earth and atmosphere   36

5   Plants and oil   32

P1a   Energy and Electricity

1   Keeping warm   40   2   Making and using electricity   44

P1b   Radiation and the Universe

3   Waves   48   5   Observing the Universe   56

4   Radioactivity   52

How science works   59

ISA and PSA hints and tips   60

Exam-style questions   61

Answers to exam-style questions   65

Answers to in-text questions   67

Glossary and index   73

How to use this book

This AQA Science Uncovered revision guide will help you revise for the AQA Science foundation exam. The guide summarises what you have learnt and links directly to the AQA Science specification.

This revision guide is divided into six units: B1a, B1b, C1a, C1b, P1a and P1b. Each unit is broken down into separate sections. For example, B1a consists of Section 1: Body conditions and health and Section 2: Drugs and disease.

Each section starts with a list of learning outcomes covering the key parts of the section. This will help you to focus on what you need to revise.

After revising this section, you should be able...

● to explain what elements are and what atoms are made of

● to describe how atoms react to form compounds

You will find in-text questions throughout the text to help you to check your understanding. Test yourself as you revise each section. If you get them all correct, move on. If not, make a note to go back and revise that section again. We have given you the answers to the questions on page 67.

Question

4 *Suggest another simple hygiene measure to reduce the spread of infection in hospitals.*

Key words are shown in **bold** and key equations are highlighted. The key words also appear together with a definition in a combined glossary and index at the end of the revision guide.

$$CaO + H_2O \rightarrow Ca(OH)_2$$

The exam will ask you to incorporate ideas about 'How science works' into your answers. Parts of questions may address How science works, subject content or a blend of both. The How science works boxes will help you apply this thinking to your answers. Remember that you should be continually questioning how scientists collect data and use evidence.

How science works

What steps can individuals and governments take to decrease people's energy consumption in the home?

Page 59 gives an example of how How science works could be used during an investigation and the questions you need to think about.

Exam tips highlight common mistakes and give you advice about exam preparation so you can achieve better grades.

Exam tip

Do not mention the ozone layer – carbon dioxide and methane do not affect this.

We have included lots of simple, full colour diagrams and concept maps to help you revise and to make the content more digestible.

The revision guide is based on the new specification and the example exam questions (page 61) will give you valuable preparation for the exam. The answers that follow allow you to check your progress and improve next time!

ISA and PSA hints and tips (page 60) is a helpful reminder of the method you should use during any investigation. This will be useful when answering questions in the exam.

Revision and exam advice

You will get the most out of this guide by using the in-text questions and exam questions to check that you understand the content. Take note of the exam tips – they will help you to avoid mistakes other students have made in the past!

You may find these revision tips useful:

- Revise regularly – do *not* leave revision until near the exam.
- Plan your revision carefully – this will help you avoid a last minute rush.
- Revise in a quiet room – you cannot revise properly with the television on or if you are listening to music.
- Revise in short stretches – work for half an hour, have a breather for ten minutes, then start again. You should be able to revise for about 2–3 hours in an evening.
- Make your revision 'active' – read a topic, then close your book and make a summary from memory. Go back and see what is missing from your summary.
- Try to get plenty of exercise and enough sleep before the exam – you will be more alert.

During the exam:

- Read the question carefully – circle the key words and make sure you know what you are being asked to do.
- Look at the number of marks allocated to decide how long to spend on a question. If three marks are given then you need to make three relevant points to gain full marks. When you are answering the example exam questions, number the points you have made '1', '2' and so on.
- Look at how much space has been left for the answer. One line means you only need to give a short answer. If there is a blank space you may be expected to draw a diagram.
- Use scientific terminology in your answers wherever possible.
- Quote the equation and show your working when doing calculations. Remember to include a unit for your answer!
- Draw diagrams and graphs carefully in pencil and label them.

Good luck with your exams!

After revising this section, you should be able...

- to describe the role of the nervous system in perception and the response to stimuli
- to describe the role of hormones in regulating processes, including the menstrual cycle and fertility
- to explain the importance of diet and exercise for health
- to evaluate claims made by manufacturers of sports drinks, slimming products and other health products

Receptors

We can sense many things about our environment:

- light
- sound
- changes in our position
- touch
- pressure
- pain
- hot and cold temperature
- the smell and taste of some chemicals.

A change in the environment that we can sense is called a **stimulus** (plural: stimuli).

Question

1 Give examples of situations where you might detect each stimulus listed above.

We detect stimuli with special cells called **receptors** in our eyes, ears, skin, etc.

How science works

Stimuli such as pain are unpleasant. Do you think we get any benefit from them?

The nervous system

Impulses from a receptor travel to the brain. The brain controls how we respond. For example, it might send impulses to a muscle to make it move.

These impulses travel along special cells called **neurones**. Neurones are often found in groups called **nerves**.

Exam tip

Remember: information is carried as impulses. Do *not* write 'messages' or 'signals'.

The network of nerves and the brain is called the nervous system. The brain and spinal cord form the **central nervous system**.

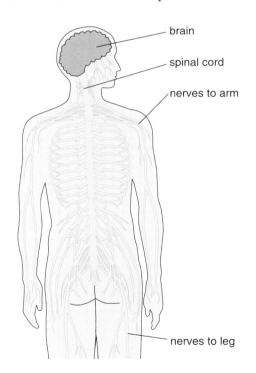

brain

spinal cord

nerves to arm

nerves to leg

Reflexes

When you touch a hot object, your hand jerks away. When a bright light flashes, you blink. Rapid automatic responses like these are called **reflex actions**.

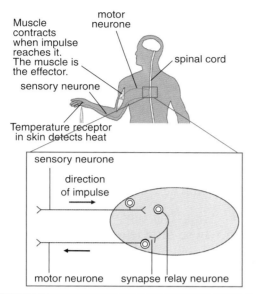

Part of body	Function
receptor	detects stimulus
sensory neurone	carries impulses *to* central nervous system
relay neurone	carries impulses *within* central nervous system
motor neurone	carries impulses *from* central nervous system, e.g. to muscles or glands
synapse	the gap between one neurone and the next
effector	the part of the body that responds to impulses, e.g. the muscle that pulls your hand away from the heat, or a gland

Exam tip

Remember: receptors *sense* the stimulus and send impulses through *sensory* neurones. *Relay* neurones *relay* impulses within the nervous system. The impulses from *motor* neurones may put the body into *motion*.

The controlled body

Conditions within the body are tightly controlled, including:

- temperature – to provide the right conditions for the **enzymes** that regulate reactions in cells

- the level of sugar in the blood – to provide a constant energy supply for the cells
- water content (shown in the diagram)
- concentrations of ions.

Question

2 *Suggest what would happen if the body did not control its temperature.*

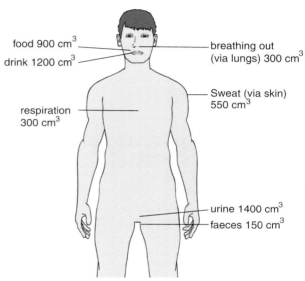

▲ A balanced water budget.

Different sports drinks contain different concentrations of ions and sugar dissolved in water. We can also get these substances from our diet in other ways.

Question

3 *An athlete drinks a sports drink after running on a hot day. Should he choose a drink high in ions or a drink low in ions? Why?*

Hormones

Many processes in the body are controlled by **hormones**. Hormones are made in one part of the body but act on a different part. They are secreted (released) by organs called glands.

The bloodstream carries hormones to their target. The similarities and differences between hormones and nerve impulses are summarised in the diagram.

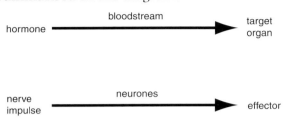

The menstrual cycle

The **menstrual cycle** takes place in the ovaries and womb of a woman roughly every 28 days from puberty till the age of about 50. Each cycle takes about 28 days.

Hormone	Secreting gland	Place of action	Functions
FSH	pituitary gland (at base of brain)	ovaries	causes eggs to mature stimulates ovaries to secrete oestrogen
oestrogen	ovaries	womb	causes womb lining to thicken
		pituitary gland	causes pituitary gland to stop secreting FSH stimulates pituitary gland to secrete **LH**
LH	pituitary gland	ovary	causes mature egg to be released from ovary

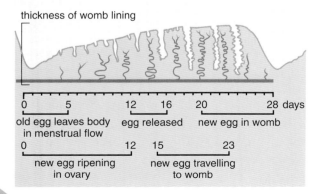

Question

4 What effect does FSH have on the ovaries?
5 Roughly how many menstrual cycles does a woman have in her lifetime?

Fertility treatment

The **contraceptive pill** contains hormones that stop FSH being made, so no eggs mature. It is very **effective**, but causes side-effects such as headaches or heavy periods in some women.

Women whose own level of FSH is too low may be given FSH to stimulate eggs to mature. This can improve fertility.

How science works

The contraceptive pill causes serious side-effects in a small proportion of women. How would you decide if this risk was worth taking?

Exercise and energy

People need regular exercise to stay healthy. Exercise increases the **metabolic rate** (the rate at which reactions happen in the body's cells). The metabolic rate remains high for some time after the exercise has stopped.

A healthy diet includes the right amount of energy to balance the energy you use. The warmer it is, and the less exercise you do, the less energy you need.

Question

6 Explain why you need less food when you do less exercise.

Diet, health and disease

A balanced diet contains the right balance of the different foods you need, as shown in the diagram.

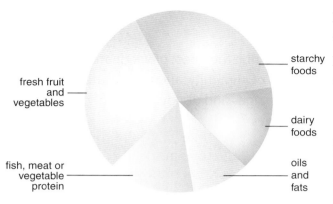

fresh fruit and vegetables

starchy foods

dairy foods

oils and fats

fish, meat or vegetable protein

Malnutrition

A person whose diet is not balanced is malnourished.

Too much food and too little exercise leads to people being overweight. This is linked with health problems, such as:

- **arthritis** (worn joints)
- **diabetes** (high blood sugar)
- high blood pressure
- heart disease.

Too little food also leads to health problems, such as:

- reduced **resistance** to infection
- irregular periods in women
- diseases caused by a lack of something needed in the diet.

Question

7 Diabetes is becoming more common in wealthy developed countries. Suggest why.

Cholesterol

Cholesterol is made by the liver and found in the blood. The amount you make depends on:

- your diet
- **inherited** factors.

Cholesterol is carried in the bloodstream by chemicals called **lipoproteins**.

Low-density lipoproteins (LDLs) are 'bad' cholesterol. They can lead to heart disease.

High-density lipoproteins (HDLs) are 'good' cholesterol.

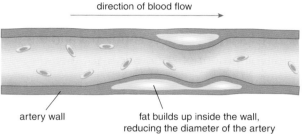

direction of blood flow

artery wall

fat builds up inside the wall, reducing the diameter of the artery

▲ Too much cholesterol can clog blood vessels.

Fat and salt

Many processed foods contain high levels of fat and salt.

Fats in the diet affect the amount of cholesterol in the blood. Too much of the wrong kinds of fat is linked with heart disease.

- Saturated fats, found in animal fat, increase blood cholesterol.
- Unsaturated fats, found in fish and vegetable oils, may lower blood cholesterol.

Too much salt in the diet can lead to high blood pressure. This is linked with medical problems.

How science works

Think about all the factors that affect our weight and health. Can one simple remedy make you slim and healthy?

Question

8 Suggest why someone who eats a lot of processed foods may be at risk of developing high blood pressure.

After revising this section, you should be able...

- to describe the health effects of tobacco and alcohol, and evaluate ways of giving up smoking
- to evaluate the use of illegal drugs
- to explain the uses of antibiotics and the development of antibiotic resistance
- to describe the effect of vaccination in terms of immunity, and to evaluate the advantages and disadvantages of particular vaccines

Drugs

A drug is a chemical that affects our body chemistry.

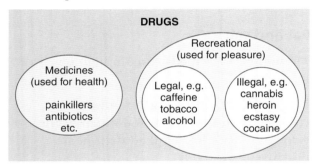

▲ Drugs may be medicinal or recreational, legal or illegal.

Testing medicines

Medicines can help cure disease or make people feel better. Before new medicines can be sold, they go through several stages of testing, as shown in the diagrams below.

Question

1 Suggest why drugs are tested in the lab before undergoing clinical trials on humans.

Proper testing is vital. **Thalidomide** was used from about 1957 to 1961 to treat morning sickness in pregnant women. But it had not been developed for this use, and had not been tested on pregnant animals. Thousands of babies born to these women were born with severe disabilities such as abnormal limbs.

How science works

Could there have been any benefit from testing thalidomide on pregnant animals?

Now, after more tests, thalidomide is used to treat leprosy. But it should not be taken in pregnancy.

Statins are drugs that lower the amount of cholesterol in the blood. They have been properly tested and found to be safe. Statins could save lives by preventing heart attacks.

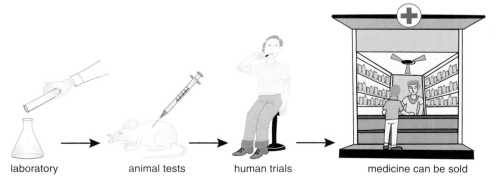

laboratory   animal tests   human trials   medicine can be sold

Why take non-medical drugs?

People take recreational drugs to change their mood.

- Caffeine (in tea, coffee and some soft drinks) and nicotine (in tobacco) make people feel alert.
- Alcohol, cannabis and heroin make people feel relaxed.

But drugs also damage health.

- Alcohol slows the reactions and causes loss of self-control or even loss of consciousness. It eventually damages the brain and liver.
- Tobacco smoke contains **carcinogens** (substances that cause cancer).
- Tobacco smoke contains **carbon monoxide**, which prevents red blood cells from carrying oxygen. In pregnant women, this deprives the fetus of oxygen and can lead to underweight babies, as shown in the diagram below.

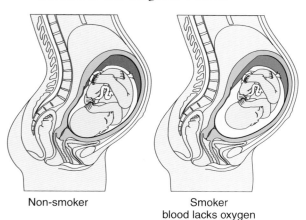

Non-smoker

Smoker
blood lacks oxygen
fetus underdeveloped

- Cannabis has been linked with severe mental illness in some people. Some cannabis users go on to use more addictive drugs such as heroin.
- Heroin damages organs, including blood vessels, the heart and the brain.

- Drugs change the chemical processes in the body. People may become **addicted** to a drug, so that when they stop taking it they suffer **withdrawal symptoms** and feel ill. Nicotine and alcohol are addictive. Heroin and cocaine are extremely addictive.

Some illegal drugs can be deadly. But the overall impact of legal drugs on health is greater, because more people take them.

Tobacco and disease

People have not always known that there is a link between smoking and lung cancer. Not everybody who smokes will develop lung cancer. And not everybody who gets lung cancer is a smoker.

To prove the link between smoking and cancer, scientists collected data from large numbers of smokers and non-smokers. They predicted that a far higher proportion of the smokers than the non-smokers would develop lung cancer. The predictions were correct. People gradually accepted the link.

How science works

Why did scientists have to test large numbers of people? Why did they have to compare smokers with non-smokers rather than just looking at smokers?

Bacteria and viruses

Bacteria and **viruses** are types of microscopic organisms, or microorganisms, shown in the diagram on the next page. Microorganisms that cause disease are called **pathogens**.

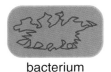

bacterium

virus

Bacteria are tiny cells. Some bacteria release toxins (poisons) which make us feel ill. Viruses are many times smaller than bacteria. They can only grow inside living cells, which damages the cells.

Exam tip

Remember: viruses are not cells, but tiny particles that reproduce inside living cells.

Preventing infection

Pathogens can be passed from person to person by coughing, sneezing, touching, etc.

The Hungarian doctor Ignaz Semmelweiss (1818–65) encouraged doctors to wash their hands between examining one patient and the next. This greatly reduced the number of patients who became infected in hospital.

Measures such as hand washing are still important today in reducing the spread of infection among hospital patients.

Question

4 *Suggest another simple hygiene measure to reduce the spread of infection in hospitals.*

The body's defences

The inside of the body is moist and warm, and contains nutrients. Bacteria and viruses can grow there very rapidly.

The body has many ways to defend itself against pathogens. **White blood cells** defend us against pathogens by:

- **ingesting** (taking them in) and digesting them
- producing **antibodies** that destroy particular bacteria or viruses
- producing **antitoxins** that counteract the toxins released by pathogens.

membrane folds around the bacteria

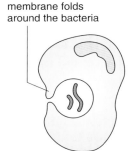

white blood cells can change their shape and wrap around bacteria

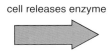

cell releases enzyme

once inside the white blood cell, enzymes are released to digest the bacteria

microbes come into contact with white blood cell

microbes

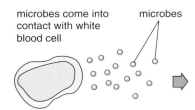

white blood cell releases antibodies

antibodies

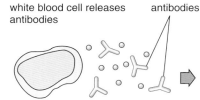

antibodies react with microbes and destroy them

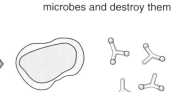

Exam tip

Remember: each antibody is targeted against one particular type of pathogen.

Immunisation

When a person is infected with a pathogen, they produce antibodies against that particular pathogen and become **immune** to it. If they are infected with the *same* pathogen again, the body can quickly produce antibodies to destroy it, as shown below.

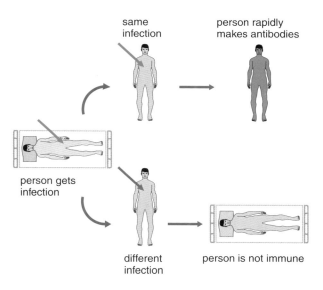

same
infection

person rapidly
makes antibodies

person gets
infection

different
infection

person is not immune

A person can be **immunised** by introducing a small amount of dead or inactive pathogen into the body (vaccination). The person becomes protected against that particular infection.

An example is the MMR **vaccine**, which is given to people when they are babies to protect against three different viruses that cause measles, mumps and rubella. The graph below shows the effect of the MMR vaccination on the incidence of measles.

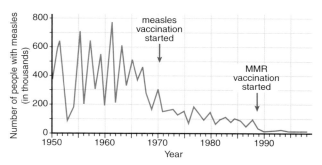

Antibiotics

Antibiotics – such as **penicillin** – are drugs that kill bacteria inside the body. They cannot kill viruses, which are inside the person's own cells.

A mutation (genetic change) may make bacteria resistant to an antibiotic. The antibiotic is no longer effective against the bacteria. Some bacteria, for example MRSA, are resistant to many different antibiotics. This makes it difficult to cure an MRSA infection.

Viruses can also mutate so that they are different from previous strains. People will not be immune to the new strain. The disease can spread to many people in the population. This is called an epidemic.

Questions

5 Explain why it is rare to get chickenpox if you have already had it.
6 Why doesn't having chickenpox protect you against measles?

Question

7 Why is it difficult to develop drugs that kill viruses without damaging the body's cells?

After revising this section, you should be able...

- to suggest how organisms are adapted to their environment
- to explain how genes and the environment influence characteristics
- to describe techniques of cloning and genetic engineering and comment on their social and ethical impact
- to interpret evidence relating to evolutionary theory

Competition

Organisms must compete with each other for limited resources.

Plants make their food from carbon dioxide and water, using energy from sunlight. They also need some nutrients from the soil. So plants often compete for:

- light
- water and nutrients in soil.

Animals cannot make their own food. They often compete for:

- food and water
- mates
- territory.

An animal that has a territory (an area of land) can use the resources there. If other animals enter, they may be attacked.

Question

1 Some plants compete by growing taller than their neighbours. How does this help them?

Adaptations

Organisms live in various conditions:

- hot or cold
- wet or dry
- light or dark.

▲ The peppered moth.

Features that help an organism survive in its environment are called **adaptations**. Some examples are given in the table below.

Adaptation	Benefit	Examples
compact shape	reduces heat loss	walrus, Arctic fox
blubber, fur, feathers	reduces heat loss	walrus, polar bear, penguin
large ears	increases heat loss	desert fox, elephant
waxy stem, tiny leaves	reduces water loss	cactus
thorns	protects against predators	thistle, cactus
camouflage	helps organism hide from predators or prey	common frog, polar bear, peppered moth, lion
poison or nasty taste	defends against predators	wasp, oak
bright colouring	warns predators about poison	poison arrow frog, wasp

Exam tip

In the exam, you may be directed to a feature of a particular species and asked to suggest why it is an adaptation. Remember that to gain a mark you must describe the feature and explain how it helps the organism to survive.

Questions

2 Jack rabbits have huge ears. Suggest what sort of climate they live in. Explain your answer.
3 The table above lists four camouflaged animals. How does each one benefit from its camouflage?

Inheritance

Members of the same species differ from each other. But offspring tend to look like their parents. For example, people with tall parents tend to be taller than average themselves.

Many **characteristics** are inherited (passed from parents to children). Inherited information is carried by **genes** that are carried by **chromosomes** found in the nucleus of each cell, as shown below. Different genes control different characteristics.

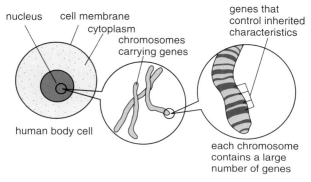

Organisms develop when their parents' **gametes** (sex cells) fuse (join together). In animals, these are the male's **sperm** and the female's **egg**.

How science works

How do you think the invention of the microscope changed biology?

Question

4 Use ideas about genes, chromosomes and gametes to explain why offspring resemble their parents.

Genes and environment

Genes influence many characteristics, including:

- height and weight
- skin colour
- flower colour in plants.

But genes do not control these characteristics on their own. The environment an individual lives in has an influence too. For example, weight is affected by diet as well as by genes.

Exam tip

Remember: *both* genes *and* environment influence the characteristics of organisms.

Question

5 Suggest a feature of the environment that can affect the height of a plant.

Reproduction

In **sexual reproduction**, male and female gametes fuse to form a cell, which divides to produce the **embryo**. The offspring vary, because genes from two parents are combined.

In **asexual reproduction**, there is no fusion of gametes. An individual has just one parent. The offspring have identical genes to the parent. Organisms with identical genes are called **clones**.

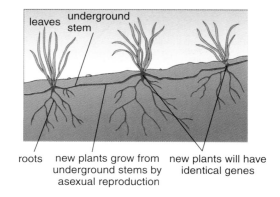

Cloning

We can make clones in several ways, illustrated in the diagrams:

- cuttings
- **tissue culture**
- **embryo transplants**
- cell fusion.

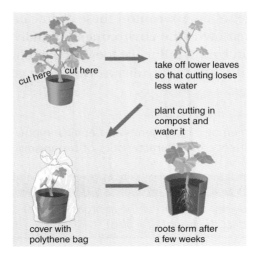

take off lower leaves so that cutting loses less water

cut here   cut here

cut here

plant cutting in compost and water it

cover with polythene bag

roots form after a few weeks

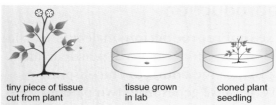

tiny piece of tissue cut from plant

tissue grown in lab

cloned plant seedling

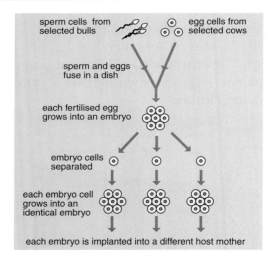

sperm cells from selected bulls

egg cells from selected cows

sperm and eggs fuse in a dish

each fertilised egg grows into an embryo

embryo cells separated

each embryo cell grows into an identical embryo

each embryo is implanted into a different host mother

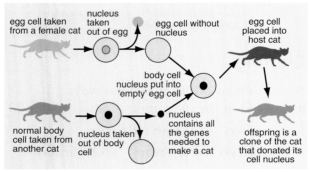

egg cell taken from a female cat

nucleus taken out of egg

egg cell without nucleus

egg cell placed into host cat

body cell nucleus put into 'empty' egg cell

normal body cell taken from another cat

nucleus taken out of body cell

nucleus contains all the genes needed to make a cat

offspring is a clone of the cat that donated its cell nucleus

Genetic engineering

In the laboratory, scientists can cut genes out of chromosomes using special enzymes. They can then transfer the genes to other organisms. This is called genetic engineering or **genetic modification**, illustrated below.

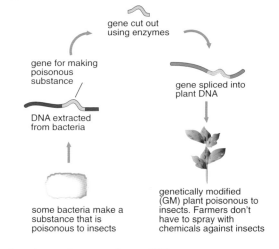

gene cut out using enzymes

gene for making poisonous substance

gene spliced into plant DNA

DNA extracted from bacteria

some bacteria make a substance that is poisonous to insects

genetically modified (GM) plant poisonous to insects. Farmers don't have to spray with chemicals against insects

▲ Creating an insect-resistant **GM crop**.

Changing species

We cannot be sure how life began on Earth. Nobody was there, and there is no complete record of what happened. But the partial record from fossils suggests that:

- simple life forms developed over 3 billion years ago
- all species alive today evolved (developed) from these ancient life forms
- over millions of years, new species are formed and old ones become **extinct** (die out).

Species become extinct because:
- their environment changes
- new predators or diseases kill them
- they cannot compete with other species.

Evolution

Darwin's theory of evolution is shown below.

Organisms compete for food

Individuals of the same species may have different characteristics, such as slightly longer legs, because they have different genes.

Individuals struggle to survive. Some die because of lack of food or may be eaten by predators.

Individuals with useful characteristics are more likely to survive, and pass on their characteristics to the next generation.

- Individuals differ because they have different genes; these differences are known as variation.
- Some are better suited to their environment than others, so they are more likely to survive and reproduce. The survival of only the best-suited individuals is called **natural selection**.
- The offspring resemble their parents because they inherit their genes.

The diagram below shows some older theories of evolution. According to these theories:
- individuals change during their lifetime. For example, an animal may stretch its neck to reach high leaves.
- individuals pass these new characteristics to their offspring. So an animal that has stretched its neck would have offspring with long necks.

But the old theories cannot work. Organisms don't pass on characteristics they develop during their own life.

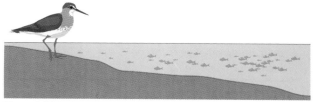

To reach fish in deeper water, wading birds stretch their legs. This makes their legs slightly longer.

Having slightly longer legs is passed on to the next generation. Birds in this generation also stretch their legs.

Over many generations, the wading birds' legs become much longer.

Exam tip

It is important to understand the difference between Darwin's theory and other theories.

Question

8 According to Darwin's theory, why are some individuals better suited to their environment than others?

After revising this section, you should be able...

- to explain how population growth leads to decreasing resources and increased waste
- to describe how human activity is contributing to the production of greenhouse gases
- to explain the importance of planning to achieve sustainable development
- to interpret data on aspects of the environment such as pollution and climate change

The growing population

The Earth's population is growing rapidly. The estimated human population for 2006 is about 6.5 billion, and it is growing by about 75 million each year.

Question

1 By roughly what percentage is the population increasing each year?

In some countries, the standard of living is also increasing: people are getting richer. As the population grows and its standard of living increases:

- raw materials are used up
- more waste is produced
- land is used for building, quarrying, farming and dumping waste, leaving less space for other organisms.

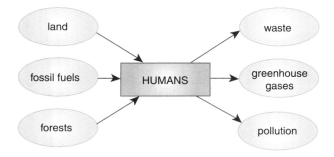

How science works

Can the Earth's population go on increasing for ever? Explain your answer.

Pollution

The waste that people generate must be properly handled so that it doesn't damage the environment. This is called pollution, shown in the diagram below and described in the following table.

Damage to...	Caused by...
water	sewage, fertiliser, poisonous chemicals from factories and farms
air	smoke and poisonous gases, e.g. sulfur dioxide released when fossil fuels are burned
land	poisonous chemicals used in farming, such as **pesticides** (for killing insects and other animals) and **herbicides** (for killing weeds); rain may wash these chemicals into water

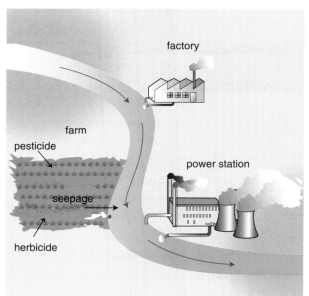

Air pollution can lead to **acid rain**. This is formed when gases such as sulfur dioxide dissolve in rain. The acid can damage trees and buildings.

Some species of organisms cannot live in polluted air or water. We can observe these species to measure pollution.

- Lichens can signal air pollution.
- Invertebrate animals such as water snails can signal water pollution.
- The worse the pollution, the fewer different species can grow.

Question

2 A river flows past a farm. Scientists count the number of invertebrate species upstream and downstream of the farm. Where would you expect them to find more species? Why?

Greenhouse gases

Energy from the Sun warms the surface of the Earth. The warm Earth emits infra red radiation.

Instead of escaping into space, most of this energy is absorbed by gases in the **atmosphere**, including:

- carbon dioxide
- methane.

As shown in the diagram below, these gases radiate some of the energy back to Earth. This keeps the Earth warmer than it would be otherwise.

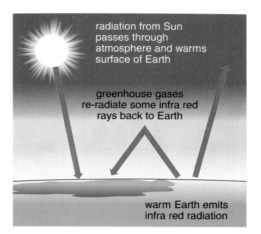

radiation from Sun passes through atmosphere and warms surface of Earth

greenhouse gases re-radiate some infra red rays back to Earth

warm Earth emits infra red radiation

Question

3 Explain how the Earth would cool down if all greenhouse gases suddenly disappeared.

Carbon dioxide (CO_2) and methane behave rather like the glass in a greenhouse. They help to keep the Earth warm. They are called **greenhouse gases**.

Rising carbon dioxide

- Organisms release CO_2 into the atmosphere when they respire (burn food to make energy).
- Plants absorb CO_2 from the atmosphere when they photosynthesise. Trees use most of this carbon dioxide to make wood, roots and leaves.

As long as these processes are balanced, carbon dioxide levels in the atmosphere stay the same.

But we are now cutting down huge areas of forest for timber and to clear land for farming (see diagram on next page).

- There are fewer trees left to take in CO_2. Less CO_2 is removed from the atmosphere.
- The roots of the dead trees are broken down by microorganisms. These release CO_2 as they respire. More CO_2 is released into the atmosphere.

We are also burning more fossil fuels than ever before, which releases CO_2.

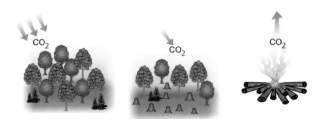

As more CO_2 is released and less is removed, the amount in the atmosphere rises.

Question

4 In your own words, give **two** reasons why levels of CO_2 are increasing.

Rising methane

Methane is made by bacteria that live where there is little oxygen.

- Rice fields are under water for long periods. The bacteria that live there release methane.
- The bacteria that live in the stomachs of cattle and help them digest food release methane.
- People are growing more and more rice and raising more cattle for food. So the amount of methane produced is increasing.

Question

5 In your own words, give **two** reasons why levels of methane are increasing.

More CO_2 and methane means a greater greenhouse effect – more energy is radiated back to Earth. Scientists think this is causing the Earth to get hotter. We call this **global warming**.

How science works

We know that levels of greenhouse gases are increasing and that the Earth is warming up. Does this prove that global warming is caused by the increase in greenhouse gases? Explain your answer.

Biodiversity

Deforestation – cutting down forests – means that animals and plants lose their habitat. Many die. Sometimes, entire species become extinct.

We do not know how many species there are. Scientists believe that most of them have not yet been discovered. So it is hard to estimate how many are becoming extinct. But one estimate is that 150 species are lost every day. Biodiversity – the great variety of living things – is decreasing.

▲ Some species at risk of extinction.

Many medicines and other useful products are made from living organisms. If a species becomes extinct, we will never know if it could have been useful in future.

Question

6 Explain why it is so hard to estimate how many species are becoming extinct each day.

Sustainable development

Deforestation, farming and building can improve our lives. But if we carry on using up the Earth's resources, future generations will not have enough.

Improving quality of life without making things worse for future generations is called **sustainable development**. It requires careful planning at many levels:

- Local – for example, communities can reduce waste by encouraging **recycling**.
- National – for example, governments can make organisations pay tax for the waste they produce.
- Global – for example, groups of countries can agree to work together to reduce the amount of fossil fuel they burn.

Question

7 Give another example of how planning can allow sustainable development. Is the planning in your example at a local, a national or a global level?

Without planning, individuals, communities and countries are not usually careful enough. People tend to think about what is most convenient now, rather than what the effect will be in the future.

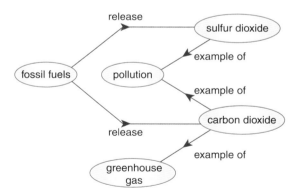

After revising this section, you should be able...

- to explain what elements are and what atoms are made of
- to describe how atoms react to form compounds

- to describe some properties of limestone
- to name some building materials produced from limestone and evaluate their advantages and disadvantages

Atoms and elements

All substances are made of **atoms**, shown in the diagram below. They are far too small to see, even with a microscope.

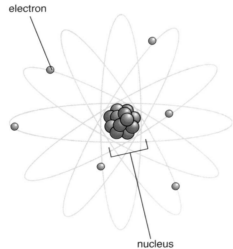

electron

nucleus

▲ Atoms have a small **nucleus** in the middle, surrounded by tiny **electrons**.

There are about 100 different types of atoms. Substances made from only one type of atom are called elements. Each type of atom has a symbol. Some common ones are given in the table below.

The symbol...	...represents an atom of...
Ca	calcium
C	carbon
O	oxygen
Na	sodium
Cl	chlorine
H	hydrogen

The periodic table shows the different types of atoms in a logical way. Elements in the same group (column of the table) have similar properties.

Reactions and compounds

As shown in the diagrams below, elements can react with each other to form compounds by:

- giving electrons
- receiving electrons
- sharing electrons.

When elements react in this way, their atoms are joined by **chemical bonds**.

▼ a) Sodium gives an electron to chlorine. b) Hydrogen and oxygen share electrons.

(a)

(b)

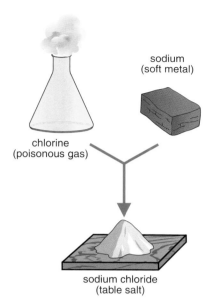

▲ Compounds are very different from the elements that make them up.

sodium (soft metal)

chlorine (poisonous gas)

sodium chloride (table salt)

How science works

Why couldn't science explain chemical reactions until scientists understood what atoms are made of?

Formulae and equations

The formula of a compound shows the number and type of atoms that make up the compound. For example, the formula for sodium chloride is NaCl. One sodium (Na) atom has reacted with one chlorine (Cl) atom.

We can represent reactions using equations in words or symbols. For example:

copper oxide + carbon → copper + carbon dioxide

$$2CuO + C \rightarrow 2Cu + CO_2$$

Equations show:

- the types of atoms that took part in a reaction
- how many of each type of atom there were.

For example, in the equation above:

- CuO contains 1 copper atom and 1 oxygen atom
- $2CuO$ means two lots of CuO, that is 2 copper atoms and 2 oxygen atoms
- CO_2 contains 1 carbon atom and 2 oxygen atoms.

Questions

1 How many atoms of nitrogen and how many of oxygen are there in (a) NO (b) N_2O (c) NO_2?
2 How many atoms of iron and how many of oxygen are there in (a) $4FeO$ (b) Fe_3O_4 (c) $2Fe_3O_4$?

Balanced equations

Look at how many atoms of each type there are on each side of the equation.

$$2CuO + C \rightarrow 2Cu + CO_2$$

Type of atom	Number on left	Number on right of equation
Cu	2	2
C	1	1
O	2	2

No atoms are lost or made during the reaction. The numbers are the same on both sides of the equation. We say that the equation is balanced.

Question

3 Draw a similar table showing the number of each type of atom on each side of the equation: $2Fe_2O_3 + 3C \rightarrow 4Fe + 3CO_2$. Is the equation balanced? Explain your answer.

Limestone

Limestone is a common type of rock. It can be quarried (dug out of the ground) in many parts of the UK and the rest of the world.

Limestone is made from calcium carbonate (CaCO₃), shown in the diagram below.

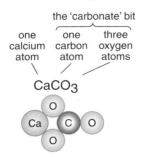

the 'carbonate' bit

one calcium atom | one carbon atom | three oxygen atoms

$CaCO_3$

Limestone is very strong, so it is useful as a building material. Many old buildings are built from limestone. It is also used for constructing roads, and for making many other materials.

Quicklime and slaked lime

If you heat limestone strongly, it breaks down.

calcium carbonate	→	calcium oxide	+	carbon dioxide
$CaCO_3$	→	CaO	+	CO_2

How science works

A scientist heats calcium carbonate and it breaks down. Explain why the calcium oxide is easier to detect than the carbon dioxide.

Breaking a compound by heating it is called **thermal decomposition**. Many other metal carbonates break down in the same way on heating.

Questions

4 Write down this equation in words.
$Na_2CO_3 \rightarrow Na_2O + CO_2$

5 What compounds do you get when you heat copper carbonate strongly?

Calcium oxide is also called **quicklime**. It reacts with water to give calcium hydroxide or **slaked lime**.

$$CaO + H_2O \rightarrow Ca(OH)_2$$

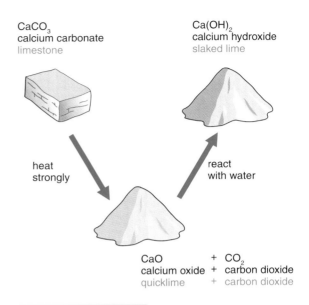

$CaCO_3$
calcium carbonate
limestone

$Ca(OH)_2$
calcium hydroxide
slaked lime

heat strongly

react with water

CaO + CO_2
calcium oxide + carbon dioxide
quicklime + carbon dioxide

Exam tip

The diagram shows just two reactions. If you learn them, you will already know a lot about the chemistry of limestone.

Cement and concrete

Cement is a grey powder, made in a kiln (shown below). Cement is made by:
- mixing crushed limestone and clay
- heating strongly
- grinding the product into a fine powder.

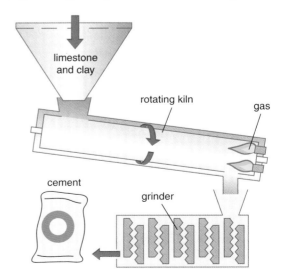

limestone and clay

rotating kiln

gas

cement

grinder

Most cement is used for making **concrete**. Concrete is made from:

- cement
- sand
- gravel
- water.

The cement sticks the other materials together. When concrete is mixed, it is a thick liquid. It can be poured or moulded into any shape. When it sets, it is as hard as rock.

How science works

Think about the gas released when limestone is heated strongly. Can you see why making concrete could contribute to global warming?

Concrete is used for making bridges, roads and buildings. It has advantages and disadvantages compared with limestone.

Concrete	Limestone
can be reinforced to prevent cracks	cannot be reinforced
can be transported as powder and mixed on site	must be transported as blocks or chips
can be moulded to any shape	hard to shape
manufactured – this requires a lot of energy	occurs naturally
appearance not suitable for repairing or extending old stone buildings	suitable for repairs or extensions that must match old stone buildings

Question

6 Explain why concrete can be made into any shape.

Mortar

Mortar is the 'glue' that is used to stick bricks or stones together in buildings.

Mortar used to be made from a paste of slaked lime and water. But that kind of mortar is not very strong. Nowadays, mortar is usually made from cement, sand and water. Slaked lime may be added to make the paste more flexible.

Question

7 How is mortar made with cement better than mortar made from slaked lime?

Glass

Sand contains silicon dioxide (SiO_2). If you heat sand and limestone together strongly, they react to form calcium silicate, which is the main compound in glass.

We can write the same reaction using everyday names, chemical names or formulae:

limestone + sand → glass + waste gas

calcium carbonate + silicon dioxide → calcium silicate + carbon dioxide

$$CaCO_3 + SiO_2 \rightarrow CaSiO_3 + CO_2$$

Glass is extremely useful because it is transparent. But it is also brittle – it breaks easily. Glass can be toughened or reinforced to make it stronger. Some of the uses of glass are illustrated below.

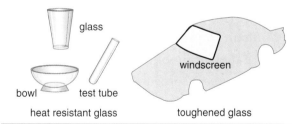

glass

bowl   test tube

heat resistant glass

windscreen

toughened glass

Question

8 Give one advantage and one disadvantage of glass as a building material compared with concrete.

Exam tip

Go back over this section and write a list of all the chemical formulae. For each formula, write down the types of atom it contains, and how many of each.

After revising this section, you should be able...

- to describe some properties of iron, copper, gold, aluminium and titanium and explain how each one is exploited
- to explain the properties and uses of alloys, in particular steel
- to evaluate the social, economic and environmental impacts of extracting and recycling metals

Useful metals

Metals have many useful properties, as shown in the following table.

Property	Example
strength	bridge
hardness	scissors
ability to be pressed or hammered into shape	
high melting point	
heat conduction	
electrical conduction	

Question

1 Copy and complete the table.

Metals also have limitations:

- high cost, because they are rare or difficult to produce
- pure metals are often too soft to be useful
- some metals corrode (rust)
- they can cause pollution.

▲ This sword is badly corroded.

Metals in the Earth

Unreactive metals such as gold are found as the metal itself. But most metals are found as compounds. We must use chemical reactions to extract (get out) the metal.

Some rocks contain enough metal to make it economical to extract the metal. These rocks are called **ores**, as shown below. Other rocks contain small amounts of metal, but extracting it is so expensive that it is not worthwhile. This is illustrated below.

Extracting metal from a rock may be too expensive at one time but worthwhile at another time.

£ 3100   copper   1 tonne

▲ It is worth extracting copper from this rock if you can sell it for £3500 per tonne, but not if you can only make £3000 per tonne.

Carbon extraction

Metals commonly occur as their oxides. If a metal is less reactive than carbon, we can use carbon to extract the metal from its oxide.

Exam tip

Remember: any metal less reactive than carbon can be extracted from its oxide with carbon.

most reactive

titanium (Ti)
aluminium (Al)
carbon (C)
iron (Fe)
copper (Cu)
gold (Au)

least reactive

When an oxide reacts to form the metal, the oxide is **reduced**.

$$\text{copper oxide} + \text{carbon} \rightarrow \text{copper} + \text{carbon dioxide}$$
$$2CuO + C \rightarrow 2Cu + CO_2$$

iron oxide + carbon → iron + carbon dioxide

$$2Fe_2O_3 + 3C \rightarrow 4Fe + 3CO_2$$

To extract iron, the reaction must be heated to a very high temperature. This takes place in a blast furnace.

Questions

2 Name one metal that cannot be extracted from its oxide with carbon.

3 What are the products when tin oxide is reduced by carbon?

Iron and steel

The diagram shows iron from a blast furnace, pure iron, and steel. The table summarises the different types of steel and their properties.

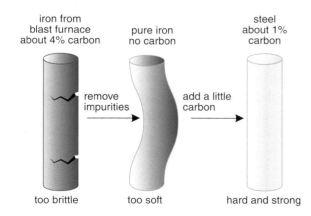

iron from blast furnace about 4% carbon — remove impurities → pure iron no carbon — add a little carbon → steel about 1% carbon

too brittle   too soft   hard and strong

Type of steel	Ingredients (with iron)	Properties
mild	carbon (up to 0.3%)	easy to shape (e.g. car bodies, drinks cans)
medium	carbon (up to 0.6%)	strong and hard (e.g. railway tracks)
high-carbon	carbon (up to 1.5%)	very hard (e.g. scissors)
stainless	carbon, chromium, sometimes nickel	does not corrode (e.g. cutlery)

Exam tip

Try to learn the name and properties of each type of steel. This will help you remember examples of where each type is used.

Copper

Copper can be extracted from its oxide using carbon. But pure copper is usually produced by **electrolysis**. This involves dissolving a copper compound, and passing an electric current through the solution. The current separates pure copper from the solution.

Copper is:

- easily shaped
- a good conductor of electricity and heat
- resistant to corrosion.

These properties make it useful for electrical wiring and pipes for plumbing.

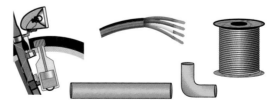

Question

4 Explain how the properties of copper listed above make it suitable for plumbing.

There is a limited amount of copper ore left. Some rocks contain copper, but in such small amounts that it is very expensive to extract. The waste rock from copper mines also contains traces of copper. Scientists are developing ways to extract copper more cheaply from these rocks.

Aluminium and titanium

Aluminium and titanium have:

- low density
- good resistance to corrosion.

Extracting these metals is expensive because it requires:

- many steps
- a lot of energy.

Exam tip

Remember: carbon cannot be used to extract aluminium or titanium from their ores.

Titanium has some advantages compared with aluminium:

- greater strength
- better corrosion resistance
- higher melting point.

But aluminium is much more widely used because it is much less expensive. Some of the uses of aluminium and titanium are given in the following table.

Metal	Use	Reasons
aluminium	aeroplanes	low density, corrosion resistance
	overhead power cables	low density so cables are not too heavy
	window frames	low density, corrosion resistance, not too expensive
titanium	fighter jets, aeroplane engines	strength, high melting point
	nuclear reactors	corrosion resistance, high melting point
	artificial joints	strength, corrosion resistance

Questions

5 Suggest why aluminium is used in electrical power cables even though copper is a better conductor.
6 Suggest why aluminium is not suitable for aeroplane engines.

Alloys

Pure metals are often too soft for many uses. We can mix them with other materials to form **alloys**.

Copper, gold and aluminium are usually used as alloys rather than the pure metal. Steels are alloys – the iron is mixed with other elements.

Alloys are stronger than pure metals because of their structures.

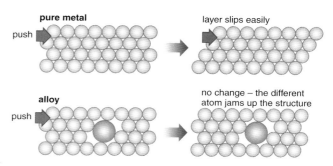

How science works

How does a scientific understanding of particles help to explain why steel is so strong?

Alloys can be designed to have particular properties. Smart alloys are a special example. If you bend a smart alloy at a low temperature and then heat it up, it returns to its original shape.

Transition metals

Metals in the central block of the periodic table (illustrated below) are called **transition metals**. They include:

- iron
- copper
- chromium
- nickel
- titanium.

Like other metals, the transition metals are good at conducting heat and electricity, and can be bent or hammered into shape.

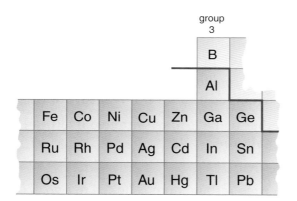

Transition metals conduct heat and electricity, e.g.

- saucepans and frying pans conduct heat
- electrical wiring and light bulb filaments conduct electricity.

They are used in large structures such as:

- trains, ships and aeroplanes
- bridges
- skyscrapers.

Question

7 Name a transition metal used in (a) electrical wiring (b) building ships.

Recycling metals

Extracting metals from ores:

- uses up limited resources
- requires a lot of energy
- damages the environment: we have to dig up the Earth to find the ore, and after the metal has been extracted, there is a lot of waste.

We can lessen these problems by recycling metals. Recycling metal takes far less energy than extracting it from the ore, and causes less pollution. But it can be difficult, because scrap metal often contains a mixture of many different metals.

Question

8 Give an example of common metal objects that are often recycled.

How science works

Suggest a way of separating the iron from a mixture of scrap iron, copper and aluminium.

After revising this section, you should be able…

- to explain how crude oil is separated into fractions
- to describe some physical and chemical properties of alkanes
- to evaluate the impact on the environment of burning fossil fuels

Crude oil

When animals and plants die, they decompose. If they are buried for millions of years, they eventually form **fossil fuels**: crude oil, natural gas and coal.

Crude oil is a mixture of many different substances. Remember that mixtures are very different from compounds.

Mixture	Compound
substances do not combine chemically	substances combine chemically
chemical properties of each component unchanged	chemical properties different from properties of individual elements
can be separated by physical means, e.g. distillation	needs chemical reaction to separate

How science works

What is meant by separating a mixture by 'physical means'?

Hydrocarbons

Most of the compounds in crude oil are **hydrocarbons**. The only atoms they contain are carbon and hydrogen.

hydrogen atoms

chain of carbon atoms

The hydrocarbon in the diagram above is normally represented as C_6H_{14} or

$$H-\underset{\underset{H}{|}}{\overset{\overset{H}{|}}{C}}-\underset{\underset{H}{|}}{\overset{\overset{H}{|}}{C}}-\underset{\underset{H}{|}}{\overset{\overset{H}{|}}{C}}-\underset{\underset{H}{|}}{\overset{\overset{H}{|}}{C}}-\underset{\underset{H}{|}}{\overset{\overset{H}{|}}{C}}-\underset{\underset{H}{|}}{\overset{\overset{H}{|}}{C}}-H$$

- Each carbon atom is linked to four other atoms by chemical bonds.
- All four bonds are used to link carbon to carbon, or carbon to hydrogen.
- The compound has as many hydrogen atoms as it can get. It is **saturated**.

Another name is for a saturated hydrocarbon is an **alkane**.

Note that:

- each carbon atom is linked to two hydrogen atoms
- there are two more hydrogens at the ends of the chain.

So, to work out the number of hydrogen atoms in an alkane:

- double the number of carbon atoms
- add two.

Question

1 Complete the formula for the alkane $C_7H_?$.

Fractional distillation

Some properties of hydrocarbons depend on the size of their molecules. For example, the smaller the molecule, the lower the boiling point.

Fuels from crude oil

Many crude oil fractions are used as fuels.

▼ Properties and uses of fuels extracted from oil.

Fraction	Number of carbon atoms	Properties	Fuel uses
LPG	3–4	lightweight, very easily lit	gas cooker, camping stove
petrol	5–11	easily lit	car engine
paraffin	10–16	safer than petrol; harder to light	small domestic heater
fuel oil	20–70	not very easily lit; safe to store; too thick to pump easily in an engine	oil-fired central heating

Question

3 Describe how the flammability of hydrocarbons changes as the molecules get larger.

Apart from hydrocarbons, many of these fuels contain sulfur as an impurity.

How science works

Remember: if you heat a liquid to its boiling point, it turns into gas. If you cool a gas to its boiling point, it condenses into liquid.

We can use this property to separate the hydrocarbons in crude oil.

- Heat the oil to evaporate it.
- Let the vapour condense at different temperatures, in a tower which is hot at the bottom and cool at the top.
- The **fractions** that condense at different temperatures contain different compounds.

This process is called **fractional distillation** and is shown in the diagram below. It does not separate the oil perfectly into individual compounds. But each fraction contains only a few compounds that are similar to each other.

Question

2 Explain why fractions with smaller molecules condense higher up the tower.

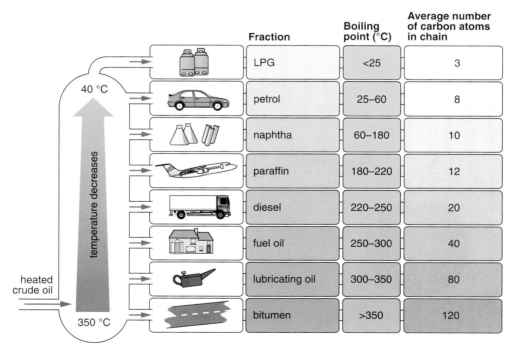

Fraction	Boiling point (°C)	Average number of carbon atoms in chain
LPG	<25	3
petrol	25–60	8
naphtha	60–180	10
paraffin	180–220	12
diesel	220–250	20
fuel oil	250–300	40
lubricating oil	300–350	80
bitumen	>350	120

40 °C

temperature decreases

heated crude oil

350 °C

Burning fuels

When hydrocarbons burn fully, they react with oxygen to produce carbon dioxide and water. For example:

$$CH_4 + 2O_2 \rightarrow CO_2 + 2H_2O$$

Exam tip

When you revise, try to link topics. For example: relate carbon dioxide to the reactions of limestone (see C1a1 Earth provides, page 18); relate carbon dioxide to global warming (B1b4 Taking care of the planet, page 14); relate fossil fuels to electricity generation (P1a2 Making and using electricity, page 44).

Burning fuels can also produce:

- carbon monoxide
- tiny particles (smoke or soot)
- sulfur dioxide.

These products affect the environment.

- Carbon dioxide causes global warming (B1b4 Taking care of the planet, page 14).
- Sulfur dioxide causes acid rain (B1b4 Taking care of the planet, page 14).
- Tiny particles cause **global dimming** by encouraging more clouds to form. This tends to make the Earth cooler.

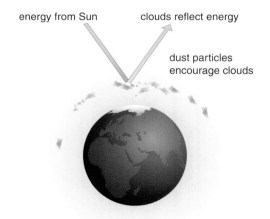

energy from Sun   clouds reflect energy

dust particles encourage clouds

Question

4 *Explain why global dimming can mask the effect of global warming.*

Removing sulfur

Sulfur can be removed from fuel before it is burned, for example in cars. Sulfur dioxide can be removed after the fuel is burned, for example in power stations.

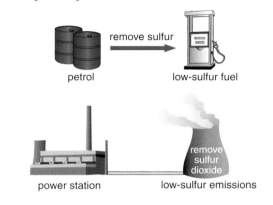

remove sulfur

petrol   low-sulfur fuel

remove sulfur dioxide

power station   low-sulfur emissions

New fuels

Fossil fuels cause pollution and will eventually run out. New fuels being developed include hydrogen and ethanol.

Hydrogen is a clean fuel, as it burns to produce water:

$$2H_2 + O_2 \rightarrow 2H_2O$$

But to make large amounts of hydrogen, we need to use electricity. Most electricity is made from burning fossil fuels! So hydrogen technology cannot yet solve the fossil fuel problem.

Ethanol can be made by fermenting sugar. Hot countries can grow sugar cane, and produce ethanol cheaply. Ethanol burns cleanly to give carbon dioxide and water.

Question

5 *Give one advantage and one disadvantage of using hydrogen as a fuel.*

After revising this section, you should be able...

- to describe how small molecules including alkenes can be made from large ones by cracking
- to relate the uses of polymers to their properties

- to evaluate the advantages and disadvantages of using crude oil products as raw materials for making ethanol and plastics
- to evaluate the environmental impacts of using, disposing of and recycling polymers

Too much oil, too little petrol

Crude oil contains a high proportion of alkanes with large molecules. These are useful, for example as lubricating oil.

But we do not need much of the long-chain compounds. It would be more useful to have more of the shorter-chain compounds, such as those found in petrol.

Cracking

Long-chain hydrocarbons can be broken into smaller molecules. The process is called **cracking**. The hydrocarbons are heated to vaporise them. The vapour is then passed over a catalyst, which speeds up the reaction.

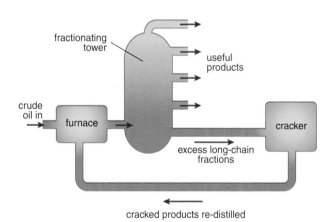

The cracking of an alkane is shown below. When an alkane is cracked:

- there are not enough hydrogen atoms to form two new alkanes
- one of the products has fewer hydrogens than an alkane – it is **unsaturated**
- the 'spare' link forms a double bond between two carbon atoms.

The products of cracking

An unsaturated hydrocarbon with a carbon–carbon double bond is called an **alkene**. To find the number of hydrogen atoms in an alkene, double the number of carbon atoms.

The simplest alkene is ethene, C_2H_4. The next is propene, C_3H_6.

Question

1 Complete the formula for the alkene $C_7H_?$.

Cracking also produces shorter-chain alkanes, which are useful as fuel.

How science works

Explain why cracking is an example of a thermal decomposition.

How science works

Why produce fuel by cracking, when crude oil already contains short-chain alkanes?

Ethanol

Ethanol is the alcohol in wine, beer, etc. It is used as:

- a solvent, for example in glues, paints, varnishes and perfumes
- an ingredient in alcoholic drinks
- a fuel, for example in lamps and environmentally friendly cars
- a disinfectant.

Ethanol is commonly made in two different ways, summarised in the table below.

- React ethene with steam in the presence of a catalyst.
- Ferment sugar using yeast.

Ethene and steam	Fermented sugar
crude-oil product – non-renewable	plant product – renewable
can be made continuously in a factory	must be made one batch at a time
needs high temperature and pressure	takes place at ordinary temperature and pressure
simple reaction, produces pure ethanol	fermentation produces a dilute solution of ethanol, which must be purified by distillation
fast	slow
cheap as long as oil is cheap	more expensive – requires many steps

Exam tip

If you picture the two processes in your mind and think about how they work, it is easier to remember the advantages and disadvantages.

Question

2 Give one advantage and one disadvantage for each method of manufacturing ethanol.

Polymers

Some types of small molecule can join together into long chains to form very large molecules. The 'building block' molecules are called **monomers**. The very large molecules are called **polymers**.

- A polymer of ethene is called poly(ethene) (often shortened to polythene), shown below.
- A polymer of propene is called poly(propene).

Cracking makes small ethene molecules

These can be made to pop together to form poly(ethene)

The chains stack up like molecular spaghetti

Plastics

The table below summarises the properties and uses of some common plastics.

Plastic	Properties	Examples of use
poly(ethene)	flexible, cheap, easy to mould	plastic bags and packaging, drinks bottles
poly(propene)	strong, hardwearing	crates, rope and carpet fibres, school chairs
poly(styrene)	can be moulded precisely	rigid containers
	can be made into foam	foam cups, insulation
poly(chloroethene) (also called PVC)	good electrical insulator	insulation for electric wires
	not broken down by sunlight	window and door frames

3 *What monomer is PVC made from?*

Slime and hydrogels

Slime can be made from poly(ethenol), as shown in the diagram below. Borax is added. A chemical reaction forms 'cross-links' between polymer chains.

● Slime is about 95% water.
● Depending on the number of cross-links, the slime can be runny or viscous (thick).

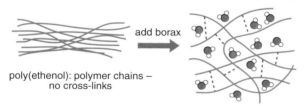

poly(ethenol): polymer chains –
no cross-links

slime: polymer chains –
weak cross-links, water
molecules trapped loosely
between chains

Don't confuse etha**nol (the alcohol in drinks like wine) with eth**e**nol (the monomer used to make slime).**

Similar polymers, but with much stronger cross-links, are called **hydrogels**. The polymer chains are linked tightly together and the water molecules are trapped. Hydrogels are used in:

● wound dressings
● soft contact lenses.

4 *Explain why hydrogels are stronger than slime.*

Other uses

Uses for polymers are being developed all the time. They include:

● waterproofing for fabrics
● non-stick surfaces for saucepans

● fillings in dentistry
● semiconductors for making microchips.

Some polymers can 'remember' their shape. If you bend a shape-memory polymer at a low temperature and then warm it up, it returns to its original shape.

Disposal and recycling

Many plastics are not **biodegradable** – they do not rot. They can be dealt with in different ways. The table below summarises some of the disadvantages of various disposal methods.

5 *The fact that plastics do not rot is an advantage for some uses. Give an example.*

Disposal method	Disadvantages
throwing away	plastics stay in waste tips for tens or hundreds of years
burning	produces smoke and poisonous gases
recycling	plastics must be sorted into different types before they are melted down
reuse	not all objects can be reused, especially if they are old and damaged

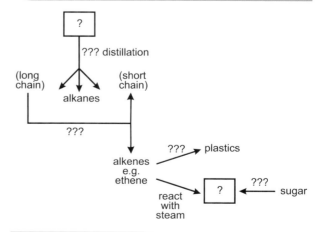

Copy and complete the concept map.

After revising this section, you should be able...

- to explain the importance of vegetable oils as food and fuel
- to describe some properties of emulsions
- to evaluate the effects of vegetable oils and food additives on diet and health
- to evaluate the impact of using vegetable oils as fuels

Vegetable oils

Some fruits, nuts and seeds are rich in oil. The oil can be extracted by:

- pressing the fruit or seed and then separating the oil from water and other impurities
- distillation.

Question

1 Name two plants that provide vegetable oil.

Oils are rich in energy, so they are important for:

- fuel
- food.

They also contain nutrients that are important for good health.

Biodiesel

Vegetable oils can be used to manufacture a fuel called **biodiesel**. This can be burned in engines that use 'ordinary' diesel from crude oil – lorries, some cars, etc.

Biodiesel has advantages compared with diesel from crude oil.

- It is renewable.
- The plants that are used to make biodiesel take in CO_2. This makes up for the CO_2 released when it is burned. This is shown below.
- It is biodegradable.
- It is not poisonous.

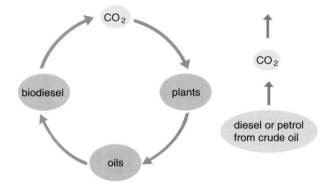

But there are problems too. A lot of land is needed to farm the plants for making biodiesel. Creating more and more farmland destroys plant and animal habitat, and farms can release pollution such as fertilisers.

How science works

How can science help us evaluate the advantages and disadvantages of biodiesel?

Saturated and unsaturated oils

Rather like hydrocarbons, oils can be saturated or unsaturated.

- Saturated oils have as many hydrogen atoms as they can get. All the carbon–carbon bonds are single bonds.
- Unsaturated oils have 'spare' bonds that are not linked to hydrogen. These form double bonds between pairs of carbon atoms.

They can be distinguished using a chemical reaction, shown on the next page.

- Shake the oil with a solution of bromine or iodine.
- Unsaturated oils react with the bromine or iodine. The solution goes colourless.
- Saturated oils do not react. The solution stays brownish.

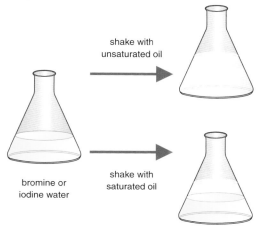

shake with unsaturated oil

bromine or iodine water

shake with saturated oil

In general:
- fish oils and vegetable oils are unsaturated
- animal fats (e.g. in meat and butter) are saturated.

Scientists think that unsaturated oils are better for our health than saturated ones because of their effects on cholesterol levels in the blood (see B1a1 Body conditions and health, page 2).

Question

2 What would you expect to see if you shook bromine water with (a) sunflower oil (b) cream? Explain your answer.

Hydrogenation

Saturated oils tend to have a higher melting point than unsaturated oils. This means that:
- unsaturated oils are often liquid at room temperature
- saturated oils are often solid at room temperature – they are called fats.

Sometimes it is useful to make solid fats from vegetable oils, for example for making:
- margarine and other spreads
- cakes and pastries
- chocolate.

Unsaturated oils can be reacted with hydrogen:
- heat to about 60°C
- bubble hydrogen gas through the oil in the presence of nickel, which acts as a catalyst.

This process is called **hydrogenation**. It turns some of the carbon–carbon double bonds in unsaturated oils into single bonds. Hydrogenation raises the melting point of the oil so that it becomes solid instead of liquid at room temperature.

Exam tip

Whenever you come across a reaction that uses a catalyst, the catalyst is simply a substance that speeds up the reaction.

hydrogen

H–H

+

---C–C=C–C---
    H H

unsaturated oil

H–H
 | |
---C–C–C–C---
   H H

the double bond breaks open

   H H
   | |
---C–C–C–C---
   H H

saturated oil

Questions

3 Explain why you can make margarine with hydrogenated sunflower oil, but not with plain sunflower oil.

4 Explain why vegetable margarine is considered healthier than butter.

Emulsions

Oils do not dissolve in water. A mixture of oil and water is called an **emulsion**. It contains small droplets of oil in water, or water in oil. Emulsions can also be mixed with air bubbles to make them smoother or thicker, for example:

- ice cream
- whipped cream.

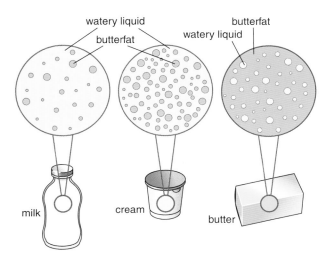

milk　cream　butter

Emulsions are thicker than oil or water. This makes them useful, as shown in the table.

Emulsion	Useful property
mayonnaise	sticks to food, has creamy texture
ice cream	has creamy texture
whipped cream	keeps its shape, looks pretty
non-drip paint	sticks to brush and walls, forms a thick layer
skin cream	feels smooth, contains oil but not greasy

Question

5 Give another example of an emulsion.

Emulsifiers

Emulsions tend to separate into an oily layer and a watery layer. For example, salad dressing separates into oil and vinegar.

An **emulsifier** is a substance that helps to prevent emulsions from separating. For example, egg yolk in mayonnaise.

Exam tip

A mixture such as an emulsion is different from a solution. The droplets in an emulsion are microscopic, but eventually the oily part and the watery part will separate. The dissolved particles in a solution are far smaller so they never separate out.

Food additives

Processed foods often contain additives – ingredients added in small quantities to improve taste, colour, etc. Some of these are described in the table below.

Type of additive	What it does	Example of food
colouring	makes food look brighter	processed meat, fizzy drinks
flavouring	adds taste	crisps, ready meals
preservative	makes food last longer	bread, mayonnaise

Many additives must be listed in the ingredients on the food packet. Some permitted additives have been given E numbers, which are often shorter than the full names.

6 *Give another example of a processed food containing (a) a colouring (b) a flavouring (c) a preservative. (If you do not know, find out by looking at lists of ingredients.)*

There can be problems with additives.

- Some people are sensitive to particular additives.
- Some additives are artificial chemicals. Some people do not like the idea of having these added to food.
- Occasionally, an additive is found to be unsafe after it has been used for some time.

How science works

Some additives, such as vitamin C and carbon dioxide, are natural substances. Should all natural additives be permitted automatically?

Chromatography and chemical analysis

Food additives can be detected by chemical analysis by the following process.

- Test the food.
- Compare the results with results from known food additives.
- This helps to identify what is in the food.

How science works

Food manufacturers test their food regularly to make sure it does not contain impurities. Why is it important for them to test several samples each time, not just one?

Chromatography is a method for detecting colours. It is done in the following way.

- Put a spot of food colour onto a piece of filter paper.
- Let water soak up through the paper.
- The colour moves up the paper with the flow of water.
- Different colours move different distances. The different colours in the mixture are separated.

There are also more accurate methods of chromatography using special machines.

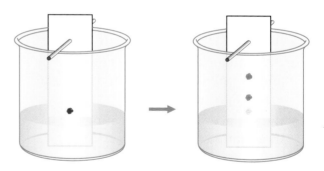

After revising this section, you should be able...

- to explain Wegener's theory of plate tectonics, and explain why it was not accepted at first
- to explain the origin of earthquakes and volcanoes, and explain why they are hard to predict
- to explain how the composition of the atmosphere has changed in the past 4 billion years
- to describe some properties and uses of noble gases

The Earth's surface

Science can try to explain the formation of features such as:

- mountains
- valleys
- continents
- oceans.

An old theory

About a hundred years ago, scientists thought that:

- the Earth started off smooth
- over millions of years, it cooled down and shrank (like a plum drying out to make a prune!)
- the surface wrinkled, creating mountains.

This theory cannot explain why:

- some continents seem to fit together like a jigsaw puzzle
- similar rocks and fossils sometimes appear on opposite sides of an ocean
- similar animals sometimes live on opposite sides of the ocean. No animal could swim this far.

To explain how animals could cross the oceans, scientists suggested that there were once bridges of land between continents.

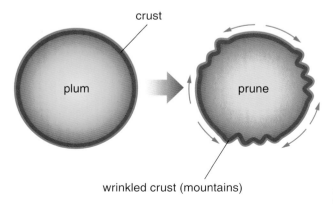

crust

plum → prune

wrinkled crust (mountains)

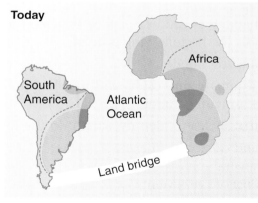

Today

South America

Africa

Atlantic Ocean

Land bridge

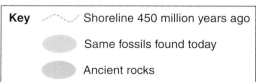

Key		
⌇⌇⌇	Shoreline 450 million years ago	
	Same fossils found today	
	Ancient rocks	

▲ Rocks, fossils and animals can match across oceans. Scientists used to think that animals crossed on land bridges.

Wegener's theory

In 1912, Alfred Wegener suggested a different theory.

- Millions of years ago, the continents were joined together, as shown below.
- Very gradually, they drifted apart.

Millions of years ago

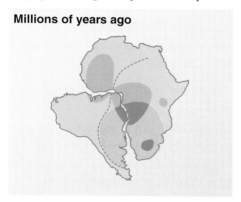

How science works

How does Wegener's theory explain the three observations listed above that the old theory could not explain?

At first, scientists did not accept Wegener's theory because:

- it went against accepted ideas of land bridges
- it did not explain how continents could move
- Wegener had some errors in his data, and calculated that continents move several metres every year – nobody could observe continents moving this fast.

Exam tip

It is important to remember why Wegener's theory was not accepted at first.

Nowadays, we can explain how continents move. And we know that they only move apart by about 2 cm each year. Wegener's ideas are now accepted because science can explain them.

Question

1 How long would it take for two continents to move apart by 1000 km?

Tectonic plates

The Earth's structure consists of layers, as shown in the diagram:

- the **crust**
- the **mantle**
- the core.

The crust and the upper part of the mantle are cracked into large pieces called **tectonic plates**. Over millions of years, they can move around the Earth's surface.

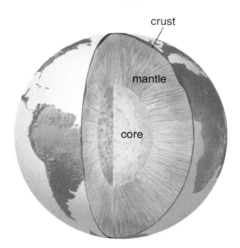

The movement is caused by convection.

- Natural radioactive processes deep inside the Earth heat the mantle so that it can flow very slowly – just a few centimetres per year.
- The hotter rock rises as the cooler rock sinks.
- This creates a **convection current** (see P1a1 Keeping warm, page 40).

Question

2 Give another example of a convection current.

When tectonic plates collide:

- they are squashed together, forming mountains (e.g. the Himalayas, the Alps)
- one plate sinks under the other at a subduction zone, shown in the diagram below.

When plates move apart, rock from the mantle rises and hardens to form new crust.

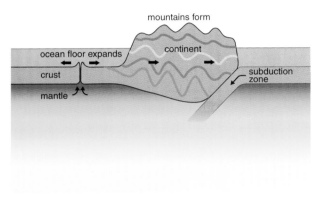

Question

3 Use ideas about tectonic plates to explain how continents move.

Earthquakes and volcanoes

Earthquakes and volcanic eruptions occur at boundaries between tectonic plates. Pressure builds up until suddenly the plates crumple or slip, or molten rock bursts out.

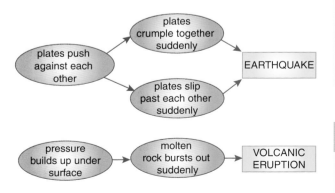

Question

4 There are no powerful earthquakes or live volcanoes in Britain. What does this suggest about how close Britain is to the edge of a tectonic plate? Explain your answer.

We do not know how great the pressure is underground, or how much pressure the crust can take before it suddenly breaks. So earthquakes and volcanic eruptions are hard to predict accurately.

Scientists can sometimes make rough predictions.

- They can try to spot patterns. For example, a volcano that usually erupts roughly every 30 years is unlikely to go for very much longer than that without erupting.
- More gas comes out of volcanoes before they erupt.
- There are sometimes small earthquakes before a major quake or an eruption.

The atmosphere

The atmosphere is the blanket of air surrounding the Earth. It provides the conditions necessary for life on Earth. It has not changed much for the past 200 million years. Its composition is shown in the table.

Gas	% of dry air
nitrogen	78
oxygen	21
noble gases	1
carbon dioxide (CO_2)	0.03

Exam tip

You need not remember the exact numbers for the composition of the atmosphere. Just remember: four-fifths nitrogen, one-fifth oxygen, plus small amounts of noble gases and CO_2.

As well as these gases, air usually contains water vapour. The amount varies.

Noble gases

The **noble gases** form Group 0 of the periodic table (the right-hand column). They are chemically very unreactive.

- Helium is much less dense than air. It is used in balloons and airships. People used to use hydrogen, but it can explode.
- Neon and other noble gases glow when an electric current is passed through them. They are used in electric discharge tubes (a type of light bulb).
- Argon is used in ordinary filament light bulbs. If the bulb were filled with air, the hot filament would react with oxygen and the bulb would soon burn out.

Question

5 Why don't light bulb filaments react with argon?

The ancient atmosphere

The Earth formed about 4.5 billion years ago. For the first billion years, the planet was hot and there were many volcanic eruptions. Gas from the volcanoes formed the early atmosphere. Some modern theories suggest that the early atmosphere contained:

- mostly CO_2 (like the atmospheres of Mars and Venus today)
- water vapour, which condensed to form the oceans
- small amounts of methane and ammonia.

The first plants evolved about 3 billion years ago, and the first animals about 1 billion years ago. As they spread, they removed CO_2 from the atmosphere.

- Plants make their tissues by photosynthesis.
- Some sea animals make shells from calcium carbonate.

Both processes use up CO_2.

These processes 'locked up' a lot of the carbon from the early atmosphere.

- Plants eventually formed fossil fuels.
- Calcium carbonate in sea shells eventually formed limestone.

As we burn the fossil fuels, we release the carbon back into the atmosphere as CO_2.

When plants photosynthesise, they release oxygen. So as the level of CO_2 in the atmosphere fell, the level of oxygen rose. The oxygen in the atmosphere today was produced by plants.

Questions

6 What is produced apart from carbon dioxide when hydrocarbons are burned?
7 Explain why animals could not live on Earth 3 billion years ago.

Exam tip

Fill in the blanks and use this concept map to help you revise.

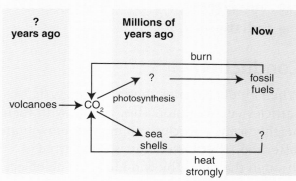

After revising this section, you should be able...

- to explain what is meant by energy transfer and energy transformation
- to describe and explain thermal energy transfer by conduction, convection and radiation
- to explain and calculate the efficiency of energy transformations
- to suggest methods for decreasing energy consumption and explain their effect

Energy and thermal energy

Energy cannot be created or destroyed. It can be **transformed** (changed from one form to another) or **transferred** (moved from one place to another).

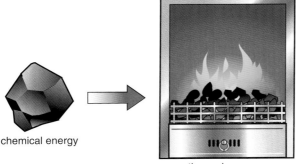

chemical energy

thermal energy

Thermal energy or heat is one form of energy. It can be transferred by:

- **conduction**
- **convection**
- **radiation**.

Conduction

When an object gains thermal energy, its particles vibrate faster. They collide with their neighbouring particles and make them vibrate faster too. Thermal energy is transferred through the object by conduction. The object warms up, as shown in the diagram below.

Conduction needs particles to be in close contact. So it works well in some solids, poorly in liquids and very poorly in gases.

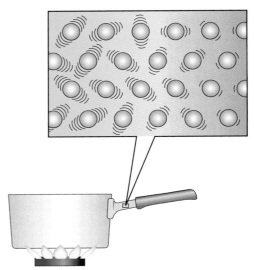

▲ Conduction in a metal saucepan handle.

Some solids are better than others at transferring vibrations because of the way their particles are arranged.

- Metals are good **conductors**.
- Poor conductors, such as plastic and wood, are good **insulators**.

> **Question**
>
> **1** Name an everyday object that is designed to be a good thermal energy conductor, and one designed to be a good thermal energy insulator. What are they made of?

Convection

When particles in a fluid (a liquid or gas) gain thermal energy and vibrate faster, they spread out and take up more space. So the fluid gets less dense as it heats up. Hotter, less dense fluid rises; cooler, denser fluid sinks. As the fluid mixes, thermal energy is transferred by convection, illustrated in the two diagrams.

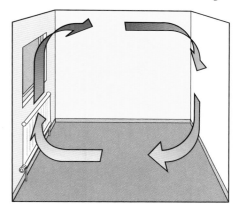

▲ Heating a room by convection.

▼ Convection in a domestic hot water system.

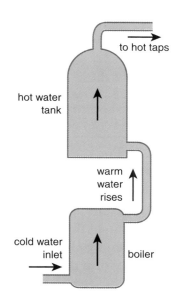

Convection requires a flow of particles from one place to another. So it works in fluids but not in solids.

Question

2 *Use ideas about convection to explain how (a) in the upper diagram, air heated by the radiator reaches other parts of the room (b) in the lower diagram, hot water reaches the hot taps.*

Radiation

Thermal radiation (also called **infra red radiation**) is a form of **electromagnetic wave**. All objects **emit** (give out) and **absorb** (take in) thermal radiation all the time. The hotter an object gets, the more thermal radiation it emits. Radiation transfers energy: when an object absorbs thermal radiation, the object gains thermal energy.

Thermal radiation can pass through a vacuum, where there are no particles. Thermal radiation from the Sun gets to Earth through the vacuum of space.

Objects emit and absorb thermal radiation only at their surfaces. Some types of surface are better absorbers and emitters of thermal radiation than others, as shown below.

- Dark, matt surfaces (e.g. black paper) are good absorbers and good emitters.
- Light, shiny surfaces (e.g. white tiles and mirrors) are poor absorbers and poor emitters.

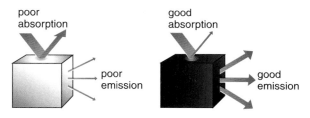

Whatever the colour of a surface, a large surface area emits and absorbs thermal radiation faster than a small surface area. For example, the cooling fins on a computer have a large surface area to help transfer thermal energy generated by the computer to the room, stopping the computer from overheating.

How science works

You are testing how well differently coloured surfaces emit radiation by making temperature measurements on metal blocks painted different colours. Name **two** variables you must control.

Questions

3 Explain why solar heating panels are painted black.
4 The ears of a desert fox are very large. Use ideas about radiation to explain how this helps the fox to keep cool.

Exam tip

Remember: conduction and convection need particles to transfer thermal energy, but radiation does not.

Temperature difference and thermal energy transfer

Thermal energy is always transferred from hotter objects to cooler objects, never the other way round. The greater the **temperature difference** between two objects, the faster thermal energy is transferred between them. For example, food cooks faster in a hot oven than in a warm oven because thermal energy is transferred more quickly into the food.

Preventing thermal energy transfer

We can take steps to decrease all three forms of thermal energy transfer.

- Insulating materials decrease conduction. An oven glove allows you to pick up the hot pan safely.
- Stopping circulation of fluids decreases convection. Loft insulation helps to stop warm air rising through the roof.
- Light or shiny surfaces decrease emission and absorption of radiation. Pale seat covers in a car help to stop the seats getting too hot in the sun.

The vacuum flask shown below has features to decrease all the forms of energy transfer:

- a vacuum between the thin glass walls to prevent conduction and convection

- a narrow top to decrease convection
- a layer of silver between the glass walls to decrease radiation.

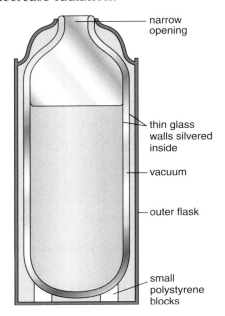

narrow opening

thin glass walls silvered inside

vacuum

outer flask

small polystyrene blocks

Question

5 Think of other devices for decreasing (a) conduction (b) convection (c) radiation. Explain how your examples work.

Useful energy and wasted energy

A light bulb takes in electrical energy and transforms some of it into light energy. But it also transforms some of the electrical energy into thermal energy, which we do not need. We call the form of energy that we want **useful energy**; all the rest is **wasted energy**.

An electric bar fire also transforms electrical energy into heat and light. But in this case, the heat is useful and the light is wasted.

Question

6 What are the useful and wasted forms of energy output from (a) a car (b) a candle (c) a television? What is the input form of energy for each device?

Efficiency

Whenever we transform energy, some of it is wasted. The more of the input energy a device transforms usefully – and the less it wastes – the more **efficient** it is. Below are diagrams of efficient and inefficient machines.

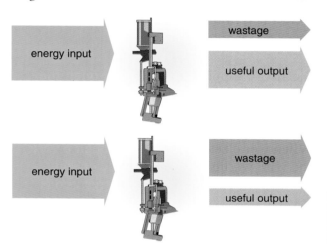

▲ The upper device is more efficient than the lower one. It transforms more energy usefully and wastes less.

$$\text{Efficiency} = \frac{\text{useful output energy}}{\text{total input energy}}$$

For example, imagine that an electric motor transforms 500 J electrical energy into 350 J kinetic energy, 100 J thermal energy and 50 J sound energy. The form we want is kinetic energy. So:

$$\begin{aligned}
\text{Efficiency} &= \frac{\text{useful output energy}}{\text{total input energy}} \\
&= \frac{350\,\text{J}}{500\,\text{J}} \\
&= 0.7
\end{aligned}$$

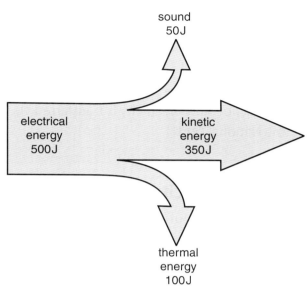

Decreasing energy consumption

We can conserve energy by slowing down thermal energy transfer (e.g. double glazing, loft insulation) and by using energy-efficient appliances.

Some methods of conserving energy are more expensive than others. And some methods save more money than others. For some methods, it takes a long time for the savings to make up for the cost. For others, the savings quickly make up for the cost. The methods that give the greatest saving for the least cost are most **cost-effective**.

After revising this section, you should be able...

- to explain why electricity is so useful and give examples of energy transformations carried out by electrical devices
- to describe how electricity is transferred via the National Grid
- to perform calculations involving the power of electrical devices and the cost of electricity
- to describe various methods of generating electricity and evaluate their advantages and disadvantages

Useful electricity

Electricity is a useful form of energy because:

- it is easy to transfer across large distances
- it can be transferred without moving large amounts of mass.

Electrical devices transform electricity into other forms of energy:

- kinetic
- thermal
- light
- sound.

Question

1 Name two devices that carry out each of the energy transformations listed above.

There is often a choice of devices to carry out the same energy transformation. We can choose the most suitable one for our needs. For example:

- a low-power electric heater is cheap to run and can stop water pipes from freezing but cannot heat a whole room
- a high-power electric bar fire can heat a whole room but is more expensive to run.

The National Grid

Electricity is generated in **power stations**. It is transferred to users along wires. The network of wires all over the country is called the **National Grid**.

Electricity supplied to houses through the National Grid is called mains electricity.

Transformers

Whenever electricity passes through a wire, the wire warms up. Some of the energy is transformed into thermal energy and is wasted.

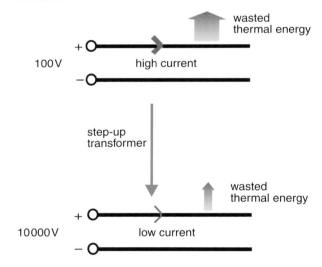

- The lower the current, the less energy is wasted in this way.
- We can lower the current by raising the voltage at which the electricity is transferred.
- The National Grid uses very high voltages in order to reduce current.
- We need to lower the voltage again for using the electricity in houses because very high voltages are too dangerous.

Voltage is raised and lowered using **transformers**.

- **Step-up transformers** increase voltage.
- **Step-down transformers** decrease voltage.

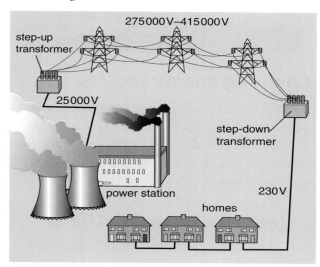

Question

2 Explain (a) the advantage of transferring electricity at high voltage in the National Grid (b) the advantage of using a lower voltage in homes.

Exam tip

Make sure you can label parts of the National Grid on a diagram.

Power

Different devices transform electricity at different rates. The more energy a device transforms per second, the higher its **power**.

Power is measured in watts (W). 1000 watts is 1 kilowatt (kW).

How science works

'Kilo-' at the start of a word always means a thousand.

The amount of electrical energy a device transfers from the mains depends on:

- its power
- how long it is switched on.

Energy is often measured in joules (J). But when we measure the energy transformed by an electrical device, we usually measure it in kilowatt-hours (kWh).

Energy transferred (kWh) = power (kW) × time (h)

Exam tip

Remember to use the right units in this equation! Power in kilowatts (not watts); time in hours (not minutes or seconds).

Question

3 How much energy is transferred by (a) a 3 kW heater switched on for 2 hours (b) a 2000 W iron switched on for 30 minutes?

Paying for electricity

On an electricity bill, 1 kWh of electricity is called a 'unit'.

The electricity meter shows how many units have been used.

Total cost (p) = number of units used × price per unit (p)

Questions

1 June 2005

1 September 2005

4 Look at the electricity meters above. (a) How many units were used between 1 June 2005 and 1 September 2005? (b) If electricity costs 7p per unit, what was the bill?
5 If electricity costs 6p per unit, how much would it cost to run a 2500 W oven for 2 hours?

Generating electricity

Most power stations make electricity by turning a **generator**. The generator is turned by linking it to a **turbine**, which is rather like a propeller. **Solar electric cells** produce a potential difference directly when light falls on them, with no need for a turbine.

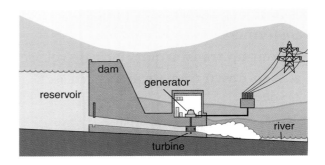

The diagram below shows some different ways of making electricity. Tidal and **hydroelectric** schemes use the potential energy of trapped water.

- Hydroelectric dams and tidal dams or 'barrages' trap water behind them.
- When a hole is opened in the dam or barrage, water flows through, turning the turbine.

Choosing energy sources

Every method of generating electricity has advantages and disadvantages. If you were deciding on the best electricity source for a particular situation, you would probably want to ask several questions.

- Is it renewable?
- What are the environmental effects?
- How much does the power station cost to build?
- How much does it cost to make the electricity?
- How **reliable** is the source? A reliable source is one that works most of the time. Sources such as wind are not very reliable because the wind is not always blowing.

▼ Different ways of making electricity.

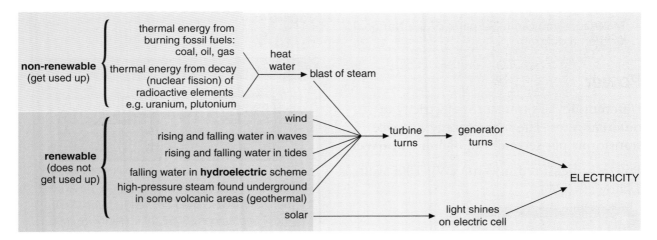

- How long does it take to start up the power station again if it has to be closed (e.g. for repairs)? Gas power stations have the shortest start-up time, nuclear power stations the longest.
- Where is the electricity needed? Some methods are easier to use in some places than in others (e.g. solar power works best in sunny climates).

The tables below describe some of the environmental effects and costs of generating electricity.

Source of electricity	Damaging effects on the environment
coal, gas, oil	release greenhouse gases and poisonous gases into the atmosphere (gas is the least polluting of these three)
nuclear	generates waste that stays radioactive for tens of thousands of years
hydroelectric	the new lake of trapped water destroys wildlife habitats
wind	can be noisy; some people find turbines ugly; turbines can injure birds
tidal barrage	affects the landscape and can damage fishing
solar	needs a large area of land to cover in solar panels

Source of electricity	Building cost of power station per megawatt of electrical power generated (£ millions)	Cost of generating 1 kWh energy (p)	Reli-ability
gas	0.4	1.5–3.5	good
coal	0.8	2.0–5.0	good
nuclear	1.5	1.5–8.5	very good
hydroelectric	1.4	1.0–7.0	good
wind (onshore)	0.85	1.5–7.5	poor
solar	3.5	10.0–24.0	poor

Exam tip

You need to be able to interpret data from tables and charts, and to know the major advantages and disadvantages of each source of electricity. But don't try to remember the numbers in these tables!

How science works

People often argue that expensive sources of electricity such as solar will become cheaper if people use them more. Do you agree with this argument? Explain your answer.

Questions

7 In the table above, the column for Cost of generating energy shows a range of estimates. Work out the average for each method, and list them in order from least to most expensive.
8 Draw a table to show a major advantage and a major disadvantage of each method of generating electricity.

Exam tip

Copy the diagram below and fill in the following methods: coal, wind, nuclear, hydroelectric, solar, gas.

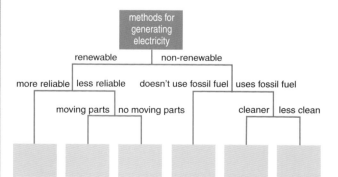

After revising this section, you should be able...

- to describe some properties of waves, in particular radiation in the electromagnetic spectrum
- to explain the uses of electromagnetic waves and relate them to the properties of different wavelengths

- to evaluate the hazards of different types of electromagnetic radiation and methods for reducing exposure to them

Waves

Waves carry energy from one place to another. For example, water waves carry kinetic energy.

Different waves differ in their:

- **frequency** (how many waves go past each second)
- **wavelength**.

Frequency is measured in hertz (Hz). 1 Hz means 1 wave per second.

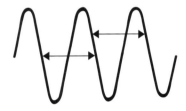

▲ Wavelength is measured from any point on one wave to the same point on the next wave. Both lines measure one wavelength.

The wavelength and frequency of a wave are related by the formula:

wave speed (m/s) = frequency (Hz) × wavelength (m)

Question

1 A 30 Hz wave has wavelength 11 m. What is its speed?

Electromagnetic waves

Electromagnetic waves or radiations are disturbances in an electric field. They all have certain things in common.

- Like other waves, they move energy from place to place.
- They can travel through a vacuum (empty space). Other waves, for example water waves and sound waves, can't do this.
- They all travel at the same speed in a vacuum (about 300 000 000 m/s).

The electromagnetic spectrum

Electromagnetic waves have a very wide range of frequencies and wavelengths. Wavelengths range from less than a billionth of a millimetre to several thousand metres! The whole family of waves is called the **electromagnetic spectrum**.

We can see a small part of this **spectrum**. These electromagnetic waves are called **visible light**.

Waves with different wavelengths have different names. There is no sharp division between them. For example, a very long microwave is the same thing as a very short radio wave.

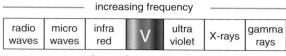

increasing frequency →

| radio waves | micro waves | infra red | V | ultra violet | X-rays | gamma rays |

← increasing wavelength

▲ The electromagnetic spectrum. V represents visible light. Violet light has the highest frequency/shortest wavelength. Red light has the lowest frequency/longest wavelength.

Reflection, absorption and transmission

When an electromagnetic wave hits a surface, it may be:

- **reflected** (bounced off)
- absorbed (taken in)
- **transmitted** (allowed to pass through).

When radiation is absorbed, it is transformed into thermal energy. The substance that absorbs the radiation warms up.

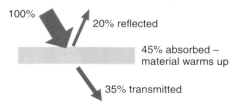

100%
20% reflected
45% absorbed – material warms up
35% transmitted

The proportions that are reflected, absorbed or transmitted depend on:

- the type of surface
- the wavelength of the radiation.

For example, window glass transmits most visible light but absorbs most **ultra violet**.

Communicating with waves

Electromagnetic waves can be used to communicate (send signals). Wavelengths used for communication include:

- **radio waves**
- **microwaves**
- **infra red**
- **visible light.**

The table below describes electromagnetic waves used in communication.

Radiation	Property	Use
radio waves	pass through walls and bend round hills, etc. reflect off the upper atmosphere to reach distant places around the Earth's curve	radio, television
microwaves	pass through the atmosphere	signals to and from satellites in space signals in mobile phone networks
infra red, visible	can be sent round curves in optical fibres (shown in the picture below)	telephone cables seeing round corners – medicine (to see into the stomach, etc.) or industry (to see inside jet engines, etc.)

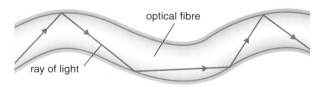

optical fibre

ray of light

▲ Light reflects off the inside surface of the fibre. If the fibre is bent, the light is sent round the curve.

Question

4 *Why is it useful that radio and television signals can bend round hills?*

Types of signal

Communications signals can be:

- analogue (varying continuously)
- digital (either fully on or fully off).

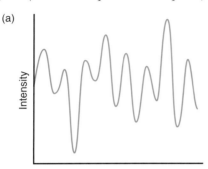
(a)

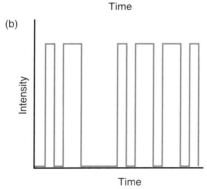
(b)

▲ (a) Analogue and (b) digital signals.

Digital signals are useful because:

- they are less prone to interference than **analogue signals**
- they can be processed by computers, which don't understand analogue signals.

So digital signals are being used increasingly, for example in:

- modern mobile phones
- digital radio sets.

Question

5 *The first mobile phones used analogue signals. Why do you think the sound was less clear than on a modern mobile phone?*

Uses of electromagnetic waves

Different wavelengths have different properties and uses, shown in the table below. In general:

- the shorter the wavelength, the more energy the wave carries.

Radiation	Uses
radio	communications
microwaves	communications; some wavelengths are absorbed by water and are used to cook foods containing water
infra red	communications, including remote-control units; infra red photography – warm areas show up brighter than cool ones
visible	seeing, photography, photocopying, scanning, etc.
ultra violet	security marker pens, fluorescent light bulbs, sun beds
X-rays	transmitted well by air and soft tissues but not by bones, metal etc. – used to see bones and other solid structures inside the body
gamma rays	can pass through metal, etc. – used to detect cracks in metal pipes; can kill cells – used to sterilise medical equipment, etc. by killing bacteria

Question

6 *Copy the diagram and fit the six words into the correct boxes.*

| longer wavelength | higher energy
lower energy
higher frequency
lower frequency
radio waves
gamma rays | shorter wavelength |

Fluorescence

Some substances fluoresce (glow) when ultra violet waves hit them.

This is why ultra violet is useful in security markers and fluorescent light bulbs.

- The security marking is invisible, but glows when you shine an ultra violet light on it.
- The bulb generates invisible ultra violet waves. They hit the inside of the bulb and make it glow.

Hazards of electromagnetic waves

Radiation	Effect on living cells
radio	mostly transmitted
microwaves	absorbed because living cells are mostly water; produce heat which can be dangerous
infra red	produces heat
visible	if very bright, can damage the eyes
ultra violet	damages cells, causing suntan and sunburn; too much exposure can cause cancer
X-rays	partly absorbed; can cause cancer
gamma rays	can kill cell; lower doses can cause cancer

People can reduce their risk by reducing their exposure to electromagnetic radiation. For example:

- people who use gamma rays and X-rays at work should use protective shields
- people should not have medical X-rays unless they really need to, especially when pregnant
- people should limit their time in the sun and use plenty of sunscreen in sunny weather
- people should never look directly at the Sun
- children should not use mobile phones too much in case the microwaves are unsafe.

After revising this section, you should be able...

- to explain what radioactive isotopes are, and describe the nature and properties of the alpha, beta and gamma radiation that they emit

- to relate the uses of different types of radiation to their properties
- to evaluate the hazards of radioactive materials

Isotopes

Atoms contain a small nucleus containing **protons** and **neutrons**, surrounded by much smaller electrons. Different elements have different types of atoms (see C1a1 Earth provides, page 18).

- Atoms of the same element always have the same number of protons in their nucleus (but can have different numbers of neutrons).
- Atoms of different elements have different numbers of protons.
- Atoms of the same element but with different numbers of neutrons are called **isotopes** of that element.

Radioactivity

Some substances emit radiation from the nuclei of their atoms all the time, whatever is done to them. They are called **radioactive** substances. The process by which they emit radiation is called **radioactive decay**.

Half-life

Radioactive decay is a random process. We cannot predict when a particular nucleus will decay.

But we can predict how long it will take for half the nuclei in a sample to decay. This period is called the **half-life**. Different isotopes have different half-lives.

We can measure how radioactive a sample is by measuring its **count rate**. This is a measure of how many atoms are decaying every minute. In one half-life, the count rate of a sample falls by half of its current value, shown below.

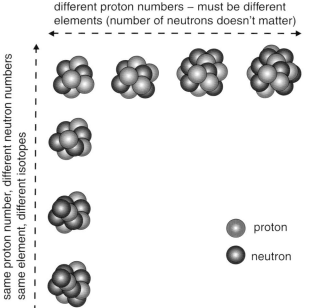

different proton numbers – must be different elements (number of neutrons doesn't matter)

same proton number, different neutron numbers same element, different isotopes

proton

neutron

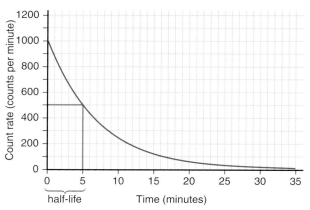

▲ It takes 5 minutes for the count rate to fall from 1000 per minute to 500 per minute. So the half-life is 5 minutes.

alpha (α)

beta (β)

gamma (γ)

How science works

The count rate falls by half every half-life. Notice that after another 5 minutes, the count rate has fallen to 250 per minute, after another 5 minutes to 125 per minute, etc.

Questions

1 The half-life of the radioactive isotope technetium-99m (Tc-99m) is 6 hours. What proportion of a sample of Tc-99m is left after (a) 6 hours (b) 12 hours?

2 A sample of Tc-99m has a count rate of 800 per minute. How long does it take for the count rate to fall to 200 per minute?

Types of radiation

Three common types of radioactivity are:

- alpha (α)
- beta (β)
- gamma (γ)

Type of radiation	Alpha	Beta	Gamma
What is it?	helium nucleus (2 protons and 2 neutrons)	fast-moving electron from the nucleus	electro-magnetic radiation
Ionising power	high	medium	low
Penetrating power: can be stopped by...	several centimetres of air thin paper	thick cardboard thin metal sheet	several centimetres of lead a few metres of concrete
Range in air	a few centimetres	a few metres	indefinite
Deflected by electric and magnetic fields?	yes	yes	no

Exam tip

You need to remember the types of radiation and their properties. Remember that **alpha particles** have a positive charge and are repelled by positively charged objects. **Beta particles** have a negative charge and are repelled by negatively charged objects.

Ionising power

Atoms that have lost or gained electrons are called **ions**. They have an electric charge. Radiation can create ions by knocking electrons from atoms as it goes through a material.

Question

3 Explain why an atom that has lost or gained electrons has a charge.

If you imagine this process, you can see that:

- alpha particles cause most **ionisation** because they have the largest mass and charge
- gamma rays cause least ionisation because they have no mass or charge.

Uses of radiation

1 Smoke detector

- The radiation source ionises the air.
- The ions create a current.

- If smoke gets into the machine, it disrupts the current.
- The machine detects the change in current and sets off the alarm.

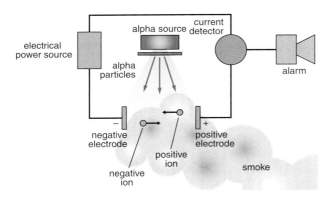

2 Controlling the thickness of paper or foil made by machines

- Some of the radiation gets through the foil.
- If the thickness changes, the amount of radiation getting through will change.
- The detector senses this change and adjusts the rollers.

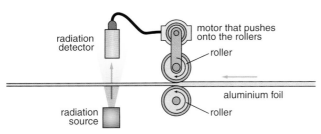

3 Medical **tracers** – used to see abnormalities in the body

- The radioactive substance is injected into the patient.
- It moves around the body.
- It can be detected from outside the body. This lets doctors see what is happening inside.

4 Industrial tracers – used in many ways, such as to detect leaks in underground pipes

- The radioactive substance is fed into the pipe.
- If there is a leak, radioactivity seeps out into the ground.
- This can be detected above ground.

5 Radiation – used to sterilise medical equipment and pre-packaged food

- The equipment or food is irradiated with high doses of gamma rays.
- This kills bacteria.

How science works

Radioactivity can damage living cells. Should it be used in medicine? How would you decide?

Choosing the right radiation source

Use	Required property	Radiation
smoke detector	ionisation (to create a current); low penetrating power (for safety)	alpha (e.g. americium-241)
thickness control	must pass through foil; must be partly stopped by foil so that a small change in thickness makes a difference to the amount getting through	beta
medical tracer	high penetrating power (so it can be detected outside the body); low ionisation (for minimum damage to cells)	low doses of gamma (e.g. technetium-99m) or beta
industrial tracer	high penetrating power (so it can be detected above ground)	gamma
sterilisation	ability to kill cells in high doses	gamma (high doses)

Questions

4 Use the required properties shown in the table above to explain why alpha, beta or gamma radiation is chosen in each case.

5 Explain why we generally use isotopes with long half-lives in machines, and isotopes with short half-lives in medicine.

Hazards of radioactivity

Radiation	Risks
alpha	ionisation can damage cells; radiation can't penetrate the skin from outside, but it can be dangerous if swallowed or inhaled
beta	can get through skin and damage cells
gamma	high doses can kill cells; this is useful for killing cancer cells (shown in the diagram below), but harmful for normal cells

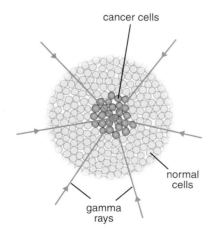

Gamma rays can be focused onto cancer cells. The cancer receives a much higher dose than the surrounding normal cells.

High-intensity radiation can cause severe cell damage and even kill people, animals and plants. This is why it is so important to deal properly with waste from nuclear power plants.

Question

6 People who work with X-rays or with radioactivity often wear badges to check how much radiation they have absorbed. The badges do not prevent radiation from getting to the body. What is the point of the badges?

How science works

You have three radioactive sources. One is emitting alpha particles, one is emitting beta particles and one is emitting gamma rays. How would you tell them apart?

After revising this section, you should be able…

- to compare the advantages and disadvantages of different types of telescopes on Earth and in space for observing the Universe

- to describe what red-shift is and explain how the red-shift of distant galaxies provides evidence for the big bang theory

Types of telescope

Space can be observed using telescopes on Earth and in space.

Optical telescopes detect visible light.

- Refracting telescopes use lenses to focus light. Lenses absorb some light, making the image dimmer. If the lens shape is not perfect, the image is distorted.

- Reflecting telescopes use mirrors and lenses to focus light. It is easier to make large mirrors than large lenses, so reflecting telescopes can be larger and let in more light, giving a brighter image.

Optical telescopes on Earth:

- can't be used during the day because the Sun is too bright
- can't see through clouds.

Stars and other objects in space emit radiation in the whole of the electromagnetic spectrum. We can use telescopes to detect the various wavelengths, from radio waves to gamma rays. Some of these telescopes can see through clouds.

Question

1 *Suggest one advantage of using a telescope with mirrors and lenses rather than one with only lenses.*

Telescopes in space

All telescopes on Earth have disadvantages.

- The atmosphere gets in the way of the radiation, making the image dimmer.

- As the air in the atmosphere swirls, the image gets distorted.

Some modern telescopes are put on satellites and sent into orbit above the atmosphere. These telescopes can give bright, clear images.

Question

2 *Explain why images from a telescope in space are (a) brighter and (b) clearer than images from a telescope on Earth.*

Exam tip

Copy the diagram and fill in as many advantages and disadvantages as you can think of for each type of telescope.

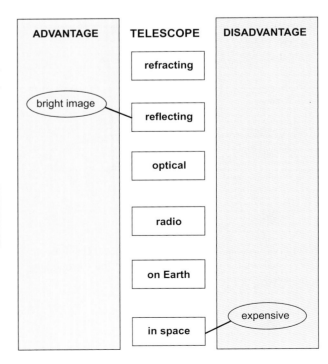

ADVANTAGE	TELESCOPE	DISADVANTAGE
	refracting	
bright image	reflecting	
	optical	
	radio	
	on Earth	
	in space	expensive

Moving sources of waves

Imagine standing still in front of a source of waves. You can measure the frequency and wavelength of the waves that reach you (e.g. the sound waves from an aeroplane).

If the plane moves towards you, the waves are compressed. More waves reach you every second. So:

- wavelength seems to decrease
- frequency seems to increase.

For a sound wave, this means that the pitch gets higher.

If the plane moves away from you, the waves are stretched. Fewer waves reach you every second. So:

- wavelength seems to increase
- frequency seems to decrease.

For a sound wave, this means that the pitch gets lower.

Exam tip

To help revise, rewrite these bullet points in the form shown in the table opposite. Also rewrite the table in the form of bullet points.

Question

3 An ambulance comes towards you, passes you and drives away. Does the pitch of its siren seem to:
A stay the same
B get higher or
C get lower?

Red-shift

The same effect happens with light waves. But because light travels so fast, you have to be moving very fast indeed relative to the light source in order to notice a difference.

When the frequency of a light wave changes, its colour changes, as summarised in the table below and in the diagram on the next page.

Source moving towards you	Source moving away from you
frequency seems to increase	frequency seems to decrease
wavelength seems to decrease	wavelength seems to increase
colour shifts towards violet end of spectrum	colour shifts towards red end of spectrum. Called **red-shift**

Exam tip

Look at the relationship between frequency, wavelength and colour. Try to relate it to the electromagnetic spectrum (see P1b3 Waves, page 48).

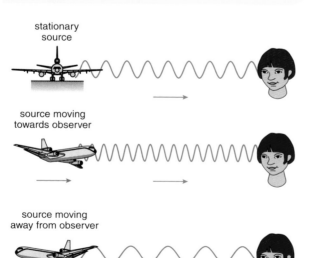

stationary source

source moving towards observer

source moving away from observer

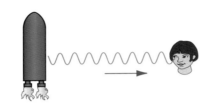

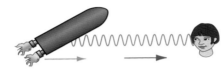

Question

4 An orange object moves away from you very fast. Will it look:

A orange

B red or

C yellow?

Spectra of stars

Stars emit a spectrum (range) of colours of light. Various elements in the star cause black lines in the spectrum, illustrated below.

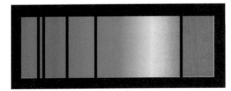

▲ The spectrum of the Sun.

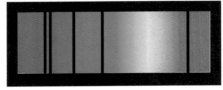

▲ The spectrum of a distant star. The black lines have shifted towards the red (right-hand) end of the spectrum.

The spectra of distant stars and galaxies show a red-shift. This suggests that they are moving away from us.

Scientists have observed the red-shift from many galaxies at different distances from Earth. There is a pattern:

- the further away a galaxy is, the greater its red-shift, so
- the further away a galaxy is, the faster it is moving away from us.

The big bang

Spectra from distant galaxies show that galaxies are moving apart from each other. This means that the Universe is expanding. It must have been smaller in the past. And at some time in the distant past, it must have been very small indeed.

The **big bang theory** says that the whole Universe exploded from a tiny point. There are several pieces of evidence for this theory.

- The fact that the Universe is expanding.
- According to the theory, a huge amount of energy was packed into the Universe when it began. This energy should now be spread out across the Universe. We can observe energy in the form of electromagnetic radiation spread out through space.
- The theory predicts that the early Universe would have produced about four times as much hydrogen as helium. The oldest stars do seem to have this ratio of hydrogen to helium.

Question

5 Explain how the observed pattern of red-shift provides evidence that the Universe is expanding. Explain how this supports the big bang theory.

How science works

Are scientists certain that the big bang theory is correct? Explain your answer.

How science works

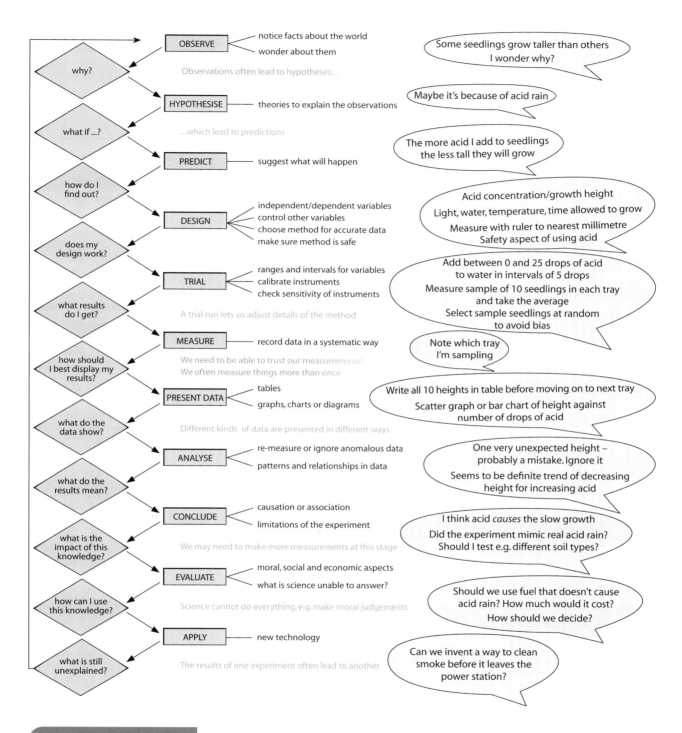

How science works

Apply the stages in the flowchart to an investigation of how the rate at which a drink cools depends on what the cup is made of. (Start with the observation that drinks stay warm for longer in some cups than in others.)

ISA and PSA hints and tips

ISA

The scientific process requires care. You may be asked about:

- whether the choice of measuring instrument is appropriate
- whether measurements have been repeated a sensible number of times
- whether the method used is able to answer the question
- whether the data allow you to draw a particular conclusion or not
- whether there are likely to be any biases.

Here are some technical terms that you are very likely to be asked about.

Type of data	Description	Example
categoric	data belong in different groups	male/female students
ordered	categoric, but can be ranked	small/medium/large
discrete	data can only be whole numbers	number of plants
continuous	data can be any number	height, weight, time

Question

1 What type of data are (a) the colour of a precipitate (b) the length of a branch?

Description of result	What it means
accurate	the average measurement is very close to the true value
precise	repeated measurements are very similar (but not necessarily accurate!)
reliable	you would get a similar result if you or another person did the measurement again
valid	reliable and also answers the question
anomalous	unexpected, not fitting into the pattern

Question

2 Bill and Jill each measure the mass of a stone three times. Bill's measurements are 92.5 g, 94.0 g and 93.6 g. Jill's are 101 g, 94 g and 97 g. The real mass of the stone is 98 g. Whose results are (a) more accurate (b) more precise?

Type of variable	What it means
independent	the quantity that you deliberately change in the experiment
dependent	the quantity you measure, which may change as you change the independent variable
control	all other variables, which you must keep constant to make the test fair

Question

3 Parveen measures how the p.d. generated by a solar electric cell changes as she changes the area of the cell. (a) What is the independent variable? (b) What is the dependent variable? (c) Give one variable that Parveen must control.

PSA

You will get marks in assessed practicals for good use of scientific methods. This means:

- using a range of equipment without much help
- taking appropriate safety precautions
- taking accurate measurements
- taking measurements in a well-organised way
- writing measurements into a clear table as you take them.

1 The drawing shows some ways in which human activities affect the environment.

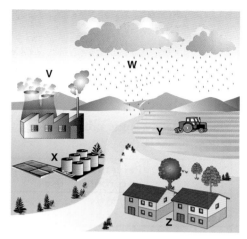

(a) How are gases produced by the coal-fired power station, **V**, affecting the Earth's climate?

....
.... *(2 marks)*

(b) Explain why the rain at **W** is acidic.

....
.... *(2 marks)*

(c) How might the sewage works, **X**, affect the environment?

....*(1 mark)*

(d) Give **two** ways in which farming, **Y**, affects the environment.

....
.... *(2 marks)*

(e) Give **four** ways in which householders, **Z**, can reduce demands on environmental resources.

....
....
....
.... *(4 marks)*

2 This question is about the hormones that control the monthly cycle in women.

(a) Use words from the box to complete the sentences.

antibiotic	contraceptives	fertility
ovaries	pituitary gland	womb

Hormones control the monthly release of an egg from a woman's .... They also control the thickness of the lining of her .... Hormones that are given to women to stimulate the release of eggs are called .... drugs. Hormones that are given to women to prevent the release of eggs are called oral .... *(4 marks)*

(b) Read the information about IVF (*in vitro* fertilisation).

> IVF gives women with blocked, damaged or missing oviducts a chance at having a baby. The NHS will fund one free IVF cycle for couples experiencing difficulty in having a baby.
>
> The woman is given hormones to stimulate development of several mature eggs for fertilisation. She is closely monitored whilst on these drugs as women respond to them in different ways and some drugs have strong side effects. The woman is given an anaesthetic and the doctor removes the eggs using a fine, hollow needle.
>
> Around 25–30 per cent of couples who have had successful IVF treatment will have twins, compared to approximately one in 90 of the general population. The national average success rate is around 17 per cent. This represents the average chance of delivering a healthy baby for each cycle of treatment.
>
> IVF has been around long enough for researchers to do extended health studies on the children conceived using this method; so far, no medical problems have been linked to IVF.

Give **two** advantages and **two** disadvantages of IVF treatment.

In each case explain the reason for your choice.

....

....

....

....(4 marks)

3 Vaccination protects us against diseases caused by pathogens.

(a) Complete the sentences about vaccination.

> A vaccine contains .... pathogens. The vaccine causes the body's .... blood cells to produce .... which kill the pathogen. These cells also produce .... to counteract poisons produced by the pathogen. **(4 marks)**

(b) The graph shows the number of cases of whooping cough notified to doctors in the UK between 1940 and 2005. It also shows the percentage of children vaccinated against the disease.

(i) Describe the trend in the number of cases of whooping cough between 1950 and 1970.

....

....(2 marks)

(ii) Describe how vaccination affected the number of cases of whooping cough up to 1975.

....

....(2 marks)

(iii) Suggest an explanation for the increases in the number of cases of whooping cough between 1975 and 1987.

....

....(2 marks)

4 (a) Explain what is meant by the term 'alloy'.

....(1 mark)

(b) The table gives some properties of different steels.

Type of steel	Percentage of carbon	Example uses
low carbon (mild steel)	0.07–0.25	car bodies
medium carbon	0.25–0.50	railway lines
high carbon	0.85–1.2	cutting tools

How is the composition of steel related to its use?

....

....(2 marks)

(c) Nitinol is an alloy of nickel and titanium. One of its uses is in 'smart fryers'. The alloy lowers the basket into the oil once the desired temperature is reached.

Suggest an explanation for this behaviour of the alloy.

....

....(2 marks)

5 Camping stoves use propane as a fuel.

(a) Name the two elements found in propane.

....

....(2 marks)

(b) Describe, in as much detail as you can, what happens when propane burns.

....

....

....(3 marks)

(c) The diagram shows how propane is produced.

Large saturated hydrocarbon molecules → Small saturated hydrocarbon molecules + propane + molecule X

(i) How are the large saturated molecules broken down?

....
....(2 marks)

(ii) What is the formula of propane?

....(1 mark)

(iii) Explain, as fully as you can, why molecule **X** is a very useful molecule.

....
....(2 marks)

6 Scientists used to believe that the Earth was cooling. As it cooled, the shrinking core made the crust wrinkle, forming mountains.

Wegener suggested, in 1915, that all the continents had once been joined together as one large continent. This large continent had then split up and the separate pieces had moved apart. At that time few people believed Wegener's theory.

Later, scientists found new evidence that suggested that the crust was divided into plates which were moving slowly. This new evidence supported Wegener's theory.

(a) Explain why scientists in 1915 did not believe Wegener's theory.

....
.... (2 marks)

(b) Explain why scientists now accept Wegener's theory. Give **two** examples of evidence.

....
....
.... (3 marks)

(c) We now know that mountains are not formed by the Earth's crust wrinkling. Explain how mountains are formed.

....
.... (2 marks)

7 Personal CD players are designed to transfer energy.

(a) Complete the sentence.

The personal CD player is designed to transfer .... energy into .... energy and .... energy. (3 marks)

(b) **(i)** What type of energy is wasted by a personal CD player?

....(1 mark)

(ii) What eventually happens to this wasted energy?

....(1 mark)

(c) A new model of the CD player is brought out. The new model is more efficient than the old model.

(i) How will this affect the life of the batteries?

....(1 mark)

(ii) Explain the reason for your answer.

....
....(2 marks)

8 Many home owners are helping the environment by installing wind generators and solar panels. A typical solar panel costs £500 and has a maximum output of 50 W. A typical wind generator costs £550 and has a maximum output of 900 W.

(a) **(i)** Over one year, the solar panel produces 10 per cent of its maximum output.

How many units of electricity (kWh) would the solar panel produce on an average day? Show your working.

....

....*(2 marks)*

(ii) The solar panel has an expected working life of 30 years.

What is the cost of each solar panel for each day of its life?

....

....*(2 marks)*

(iii) What is the approximate cost of each unit of electricity produced by the solar panel?

....

....*(2 marks)*

(b) The graph shows a performance curve for the wind generator.

Describe, in as much detail as you can, the relationship between wind speed and the power output of the generator.

....

....

....*(3 marks)*

(c) Evaluate the solar panel and wind generator as means of producing electricity for a house.

....

....

....

....

....*(5 marks)*

9 Radon is a radioactive gas produced when uranium atoms decay. Radon is formed from uranium, which is found in all rock and soil, and enters houses from the ground underneath. The graph shows a decay curve for a sample of radon collected from a house.

(a) Calculate the half-life of radon. Show your working.

....

....*(2 marks)*

(b) Explain, as fully as you can, the possible long-term effects of living in a house built over rocks that contain uranium.

....

....

....

....*(4 marks)*

Answers to exam-style questions

1 (a) carbon dioxide in gases *(1)* is causing global warming *(1)*

(b) sulfur dioxide in gases *(1)* dissolves in rain to produce acid *(1)*

(c) pollutes water in river *(1)*

(d) pesticides pollute land *(1)* fertilisers pollute water *(1)*

(e) using less energy in the home *(1)* using public transport or walking *(1)* recycling materials *(1)* using local produce / organic produce *(1)*

2 (a) ovaries *(1)* womb *(1)* fertility *(1)* contraceptives *(1)*

(b) advantages: enables infertile women to have babies *(1)* no medical problems among children produced in this way *(1)*

disadvantages: any **two** from: possible side effects from drugs *(1)* higher chance of twins *(1)* low success rate *(1)*

3 (a) dead / inactive *(1)* white *(1)* antibodies *(1)* antitoxins *(1)*

(b) (i) decreased overall *(1)* but increases in some years *(1)*

(ii) reduced overall *(1)* to almost zero *(1)*

(iii) many parents decided against vaccination *(1)* because of the fear of side effects *(1)*

4 (a) a mixture of metals *(1)*

(b) high amount of carbon gives harder steel *(1)* which will not wear as easily *(1)*

(c) Nitinol is a smart alloy *(1)* which remembers its original shape when heated *(1)*

5 (a) carbon *(1)* hydrogen *(1)*

(b) carbon dioxide *(1)* water vapour *(1)* and heat *(1)* are released

(c) (i) heated *(1)* passed over hot catalyst *(1)*

(ii) C_3H_8 *(1)*

(iii) unsaturated *(1)* so it can produce polymers *(1)*

6 (a) insufficient evidence of movement *(1)* mechanism of movement not yet proposed *(1)*

(b) more evidence now available *(1)* similar rocks on different sides of the ocean *(1)* similar fossils on different sides of the ocean *(1)*

(c) collisions between plates *(1)* forces edge of plate upwards *(1)*

7 (a) electrical *(1)* movement *(1)* sound *(1)*

(b) (i) heat *(1)*

(ii) transferred to environment *(1)*

(c) (i) batteries will last longer *(1)*

(ii) new model uses less electricity *(1)* to produce the same amount of sound or movement *(1)*

8 (a) (i) Output power = 10% × 50 = 5 W

Units (kWh) generated in one day = (output power/1000) × 24 *(1)*

= (5/1000) × 24

= 0.12 *(1)*

(ii) 500/(30 × 365) *(1)*
= £0.04566 or 4.6p *(1)*

(iii) 0.12 units cost 4.6p, so 1 unit
will cost 4.6/0.12 *(1)* = 38.3p *(1)*

(b) rises rapidly with wind speed *(1)* until
it peaks at 14 m/s *(1)* and then falls *(1)*

(c) any **five** from: wind generator
produces more electricity than solar
panel *(1)* electricity produced by
wind generator is cheaper *(1)* power
from solar cell is reliable *(1)* but no
electricity produced at night *(1)* power
from wind generator is unreliable *(1)*
because there is no wind on some
days *(1)*

9 (a) cpm is 2000 at 31 minutes and 1000
at 61 minutes *(1)* so half-life is 30
minutes *(1)*

(b) radiation from rocks *(1)* damages
cells *(1)* causing mutations *(1)* which
increase cancer risk *(1)*

B1a1 Body conditions and health (page 2)

1 Light – seeing a friend; sound – listening to music; changes in our position – balancing while walking; touch – feeling for a light switch in the dark; pressure – pushing a button; pain – cutting oneself; hot and cold temperature – holding a cup of hot or cold drink; the smell and taste of some chemicals – smelling and tasting food.

2 Enzymes would work less well so the body could not control its chemical reactions. The person would become ill.

3 High enough to replace the ions lost through sweating.

4 Stimulates secretion of oestrogen.

5 Average one per month from age 13 to 50 = 444.

6 Less exercise means lower metabolic rate, i.e. slower chemical reactions in the body. Less energy from food is used, so we need less food to replace the energy.

7 It is becoming more common to eat too much and/or not take enough exercise.

8 Many processed foods are high in salt. Too much salt can lead to high blood pressure.

B1a2 Drugs and disease (page 6)

1 It is often possible to detect in the lab if they will be harmful to humans.

2 Alcohol slows reactions and leads to loss of control. Fast reactions and good control are important for safe driving.

3 Perhaps people only think about the short-term enjoyable effects.

4 E.g. use sterile equipment for each patient and wear face mask to prevent inhalation of droplets from sneezing.

5 Having chickenpox makes the body produce antibodies to the illness. It can then fight a second infection rapidly and efficiently.

6 Each antibody is targeted against one particular pathogen.

7 Viruses are inside a person's own cells and use the cell to grow. It is hard to damage them without damaging the cell.

B1b3 Variation and evolution (page 10)

1 Taller plants get more light.

2 Hot. Their ears help them lose thermal energy so they do not overheat.

3 Frog/moth: hide from predators; polar bear/lion: hide from prey.

4 Parents' chromosomes pass into their gametes and so into the offspring. These chromosomes carry genes, some of which influence the way we look. Offspring inherit all their genes from their parents, so they resemble them.

5 E.g. amount of light, amount of water, temperature, nutritional content of soil.

6 The nucleus donor provides the genes.

7 Certain wild plants could become resistant to insects. E.g. if caterpillars could not find any plants to eat, populations of butterflies might fall. This could affect the bird population that preys on caterpillars.

8 Because they are born with different genes.

B1b4 Taking care of the planet (page 14)

1 75 million as a percentage of 6.5 billion is (75 million/6.5 billion) × 100 = 1.2%.

2 Upstream. Fewer species can grow in polluted water. This is likely to be

downstream from the farm, because toxic chemicals used on the farm could wash into the river.

3 The thermal (infra red) radiation emitted by the Earth would escape into outer space instead of being absorbed by greenhouse gases. This would cause the Earth to cool down.

4 (a) There are fewer trees to absorb the carbon dioxide and use it to build their tissues.

(b) As the wood is burned and the roots decay, carbon dioxide is released.

5 (a) More land is being used for rice production. Bacteria living in the flooded rice fields produce methane.

(b) More cattle are being raised. Bacteria in their guts release methane.

6 We still do not know how many species there are, so it is hard to estimate how rapidly they are becoming extinct.

7 E.g. local: local councils can subsidise buses; national: national government can provide grants for loft insulation; international: wealthy countries provide poorer ones with technology to reduce pollution.

C1a1 Earth provides (page 18)

1 (a) 1 nitrogen, 1 oxygen.

(b) 2 nitrogen, 1 oxygen.

(c) 1 nitrogen, 2 oxygen.

2 (a) 4 iron, 4 oxygen.

(b) 3 iron, 4 oxygen.

(c) 6 iron, 8 oxygen.

3

Type of atom	Number on left of equation	Number on right of equation
Fe	4	4
O	6	6
C	3	3

Balanced: there is the same number of each type of atom on each side.

4 Sodium carbonate gives sodium oxide and carbon dioxide.

5 Copper oxide and carbon dioxide.

6 When it is made it is liquid and can be poured into a mould.

7 It is stronger.

8 Advantage: lets light through; disadvantage: brittle.

C1a2 Useful metals (page 22)

1 E.g. can, light bulb filament, saucepan, electric cable.

2 Anything above carbon in the reactivity series, e.g. aluminium, titanium.

3 Tin and carbon dioxide.

4 Easily shaped – can be made into pipes which can be bent; good at conducting heat – useful if water in a copper pipe is pumped through a hot boiler to heat it up; resistant to corrosion – pipes need to last a long time as they are difficult to replace.

5 The cables are less heavy so they do not sag so much or break under their own weight.

6 Its melting point is too low.

7 (a) Copper. (b) Iron.

8 E.g. food cans, drinks cans.

C1a3 Oil: black gold (page 26)

1 C_7H_{16}

2 Smaller molecules have lower boiling points, so they condense at lower temperatures. The tower gets cooler higher up.

3 They become less flammable.

4 Global dimming tends to make the Earth cooler.

5 Advantage: clean, produces only water when burned. Disadvantage: explosive, so can be dangerous.

C1b4 Oil is not just for energy! (page 29)

1 C_7H_{14}

2

	Ethene and steam	Fermented sugar
Advantages	continuous; fast	batch process; slow
Disadvantages	not renewable; needs high temperature and pressure	renewable; takes place at ordinary temperature and pressure

3 Chloroethene.

4 The chains are bound tightly together. In slime, the links between chains can break and re-form easily.

5 E.g. plastic underground pipes, plastic window frames.

C1b5 Plants and oil (page 32)

1 E.g. sunflower, rape, olive, peanut, corn.

2 (a) The colour will disappear. Sunflower oil is likely to contain unsaturated oil.

(b) The colour will remain. Cream is likely to contain saturated fats. Bromine water goes colourless when shaken with unsaturated oils, but not with saturated fats.

3 Unsaturated oils are liquid at room temperature. Margarine needs to be a soft solid at room temperature. Hydrogenating the oil increases the proportion of saturated fats and therefore raises the melting point.

4 There are more carbon–carbon double bonds, so vegetable margarine is higher in unsaturated oils.

5 E.g. milk, margarine.

6 (a) E.g. brightly-coloured sweets, cake icing.

(b) E.g. soft drinks, packet soup.

(c) E.g. fruit juice, cooked meats.

C1b6 Earth and atmosphere (page 36)

1 50 million years.

2 E.g. current that causes liquid to swirl in a saucepan heated from below; air current in room heated by radiator.

3 The continents are parts of the crust. As the tectonic plates move, the continents that form their surfaces move.

4 Britain is far from the edge of a plate. Close to the edges of plates there tend to be volcanoes and earthquakes.

5 Noble gases, including argon, are extremely unreactive.

6 Water.

7 The atmosphere contained too much carbon dioxide and not enough oxygen.

P1a1 Keeping warm (page 40)

1 Good thermal conductor: e.g. saucepan, element in kettle (made of metal); good thermal insulator: e.g. polystyrene cup, insulation in walls of fridge (made of plastic).

2 **(a)** Air heated by the radiator is less dense than the surrounding air. It rises and pushes the air above out of the way. At the same time, cold air moves to fill the space near the radiator. These movements create an air current. As the warm air cools down and the new air by the radiator warms up, the current continues to circulate.

(b) Hot water from the boiler is less dense than the surrounding water so it rises into the tank. The warmest water in the tank is least dense, so rises to the top of the tank, where there is an outlet to the hot taps.

3 To absorb the maximum amount of solar radiation.

4 The fox is a mammal, so its blood is typically warmer than the surroundings. This means that the ears emit radiation faster than they absorb it, so the fox cools down. The larger the surface area of the ears, the more radiation they emit.

5 **(a)** E.g. polystyrene cup. Plastic is a poor conductor, and air is even worse. A polystyrene cup is made of air bubbles in plastic, so is slow to conduct the heat away from the drink.

(b) E.g. cavity wall insulation. Air in cavity walls can rise by convection and take thermal energy from the building as it seeps out of the wall. Cavity wall insulation traps the air in pockets. This reduces convection.

(c) E.g. white clothes. Less thermal energy is absorbed from the Sun's radiation, so keeping the person cool.

6

Device	Input energy	Useful output	Wasted output
car	chemical	kinetic	thermal, sound
candle	chemical	light	thermal
TV	electrical	light, sound	thermal

7

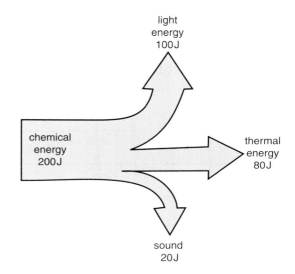

The useful energy of a coal fire is thermal.

So efficiency = 80/200 × 100% = 40%.

P1a2 Making and using electricity (page 44)

1 Kinetic: e.g. electric fan, electric toy train, electric car; thermal: e.g. electric bar fire, hairdryer, electric oven; light: e.g. light bulb, television screen, camera flash bulb; sound: e.g. radio, stereo, electric buzzer.

2 **(a)** Less energy is wasted by being transformed into thermal energy in the wires.

(b) It is safer.

3 (a) $3\,\text{kW} \times 2\,\text{h} = 6\,\text{kWh}.$

(b) $2000\,\text{W} \times 30\,\text{min} = 2\,\text{kW} \times 0.5\,\text{h}$
$$= 1\,\text{kWh}.$$

4 (a) $23200 - 22600 = 600$ units.

(b) 600 units @ 7p/unit = £42.

5 $2500\,\text{W} \times 2\,\text{h} = 2.5\,\text{kW} \times 2\,\text{h} = 5\,\text{kWh}$
$$= 5\ \text{units}$$
5 units @ 6p/unit = 30p.

6 Kinetic.

7 Gas 2.5p/kW; coal 3.5p/kW; hydroelectric 4p/kW; onshore wind 4.5p/kW; nuclear 5p/kW; solar 17p/kW.

8

Method	Major advantages	Major disadvantages
gas	low building and running costs, reliable	not renewable, polluting
coal	quite low building and running costs, reliable	not renewable, polluting
nuclear	very reliable	produces radioactive waste, can be dangerous
hydro-electric	renewable, reliable	creating a reservoir damages the environment
wind	renewable, low building cost	low reliability, turbines can damage the environment
tidal	renewable	low reliability, can affect the landscape and fishing
solar	renewable, no moving parts so easy to maintain	expensive, low reliability

P1b3 Waves (page 48)

1 Wave speed (m/s) = frequency (Hz) × wavelength (m)
$$= 30\,\text{Hz} \times 11\,\text{m} = 330\,\text{m/s}$$

2 Decreases.

3 Thermal.

4 Radios or TVs will receive a signal even if there is a hill between them and the transmitter.

5 Analogue signals are more prone to interference.

6 longer wavelength, lower energy, lower frequency, radio waves; shorter wavelength, higher energy, higher frequency, gamma rays.

P1b4 Radioactivity (page 52)

1 (a) Half.

(b) One quarter.

2 12 hours.

3 In an atom, the positive charge in the nucleus is exactly balanced by the negative charge on the electrons because there are the same number of electrons and protons. If the atom gains or loses an electron, the positive and negative charges are no longer balanced so there is an overall charge.

4 Smoke detector: alpha particles cause the most ionisation and have the lowest penetrating power; Thickness control: alpha particles would not get through the foil at all, gamma rays would get through so easily that a small change in thickness would not make a noticeable difference;

Medical tracer: alpha particles would not have the penetrating power to be detected outside the body, gamma rays cause the least ionisation; Industrial tracer: gamma rays have the highest penetrating power; Sterilisation: gamma rays kill cells in high doses.

5 In machines, it is convenient not to have to replace the radioactive material. In medicine, the radiation can cause damage to the body as long as it is present, so we choose materials with short half-lives that will quickly decay.

6 People can check if they have accidentally received too high a dose. If they have, then they can be treated or can stop working with radioactivity or X-rays for a while.

P1b5 Observing the Universe (page 56)

1 It is easier to make large mirrors than large lenses. A large mirror will give a brighter image.

2 (a) There is no atmosphere in the way to absorb some of the radiation.

   (b) There is no swirling atmosphere to distort the image.

3 C

4 B

5 The further away objects are, the faster we are moving apart from them. This suggests that the Universe is expanding.

If we imagine going back in time, the Universe must have been smaller. The further back in time we go, the smaller it would have been. At some time in the very distant past, it would have started out as a tiny point-like object. This is the big bang theory.

Glossary and index

absorb   To take in radiation. Page 41

acid rain   Rain that has been acidified by pollutants such as sulfur dioxide. Page 15

adaptations   Features that make a structure more suitable for its function. Page 10

addicted   Dependent on a drug. Page 7

alkanes   Hydrocarbons that only have single C–C or C–H bonds, e.g. ethane C_2H_6. Page 26

alkenes   Hydrocarbons with one (or more) C=C double bonds, e.g. ethene C_2H_4. Page 29

alloy   Carefully blended metal mixture with specific properties. Page 24

alpha particle   Two protons and two neutrons – the same as a helium nucleus. Page 53

analogue signal   A signal that can vary continuously within a range of values; the opposite of a digital signal. Page 50

antibiotics   Chemicals produced by microbes, used to destroy bacteria in the body. Page 9

antibodies   Substances produced when white blood cells detect the presence of a particular antigen. Page 8

antitoxins   Substances produced by white blood cells to neutralise poisons produced by microbes. Page 8

arthritis   A painful inflammation of the joints. Page 5

asexual reproduction   Reproduction that does not involve the formation of gametes. New organisms formed by asexual reproduction are genetically identical to the parent organisms. Page 11

atmosphere   The layer of gas that surrounds the Earth; approximately 80% nitrogen, 20% oxygen. Page 15

atoms   The smallest parts of an element that still have the properties of that element. Page 18

bacteria   A type of microbe. Some bacteria are useful, others cause disease. Page 7

beta particle   An electron emitted from the nucleus of an atom during radioactive decay. Page 53

big bang theory   The theory that says the Universe was created by a huge explosion. Page 58

biodegradable   Something that can be broken down easily by natural, biological processes. Page 31

biodiesel   A renewable fuel made from vegetable oil that can be used in place of diesel. Page 32

carbon monoxide   Poisonous gas produced by incomplete combustion of carbon compounds. Page 7

carcinogens   Substances that cause cancer. Page 7

cement   A powder that sets hard when mixed with water; made by heating limestone with clay. Page 20

central nervous system   The brain and spinal cord. Page 2

characteristics   Distinguishing features. Page 11

chemical bonds   Bonds that form between atoms during chemical reactions, and which hold molecules and other compounds together. Page 18

chromatography   A method of separating different dyes and chemicals such as food colours. Page 35

chromosomes   Long threads containing many genes, found in the nucleus of a cell. Page 11

clones   Genetically identical organisms. Page 11

concrete   A building material made by mixing cement, sand and gravel with water: sets to a very hard 'artificial rock'. Page 21

conduction   Transfer of thermal energy by transfer of vibration from particles to their neighbours. Page 40

conductors   Substances that are good at conducting thermal energy. Page 40

contraceptive pill   A pill containing hormones that prevent an egg being released. Page 4

convection   Transfer of thermal energy in a gas or liquid by the movement of particles from place to place. Hotter, less dense regions float and cooler, denser regions sink. Page 40

convection currents   Swirling currents that form when a liquid or gas (or very hot rock) is heated from below. Page 37

cost-effective   A measure is cost-effective if it saves more money than it costs. Page 43

count rate   The reading on a Geiger counter showing the rate at which radiation has been detected. Page 52

cracking   The process by which long-chain hydrocarbons are broken up into shorter and more useful hydrocarbons. Page 29

crust   The thin, hard and brittle outer layer of the Earth. Page 37

deforestation   Clearing of trees. Page 16

diabetes   Disorder where the pancreas fails to control glucose concentration. Page 5

digital signal   A signal that carries information in the form of a string of on and off pulses; the opposite of an analogue signal. Page 50

effective   A measure is effective if it has a great effect. An energy-saving measure is more effective the more money it saves. Page 4

effector An organ or cell that brings about a response to a stimulus. Page 3

efficiency The proportion of the energy supplied to a device that is transformed usefully rather than wasted. Page 43

efficient The higher the efficiency of a device, the more efficient it is. Page 43

egg The female sex cell (gamete). Page 11

electrolysis The tearing apart of a molten (or dissolved) ionic compound using electricity. Page 23

electromagnetic spectrum All types of electromagnetic radiation, arranged in order according to their wavelengths and frequencies. Page 48

electromagnetic wave A form of energy that is transferred as fast-moving waves. Electromagnetic waves include light and thermal radiation and can travel through a vacuum. Page 41

electrons Small particles with tiny mass and a single negative charge. Page 18

embryo transplants Transferring embryos from one organism and implanting them into another uterus (womb). Page 11

embryos Unborn offspring. Page 11

emit To give out radiation. Page 41

emulsifiers Chemicals that help stop an emulsion from separating. Page 34

emulsion A mixture of tiny droplets of oil in water (or water in oil). Page 34

enzymes Catalysts produced by cells. Page 3

ethanol The 'alcohol' in alcoholic drinks made by fermenting sugar; may also be used as a fuel. Page 30

extinct A species that used to live on Earth but which has all died out. Page 13

fossil fuels Fuels such as coal, oil or gas, formed over millions of years from the remains of living things. Page 26

fractional distillation Distillation that separates a mixture of liquids into components with different boiling points. Page 27

fractions The different liquids produced from a complex mixture such as crude oil by fractional distillation. Page 27

frequency The number of waves per second; measured in hertz (Hz). Page 48

FSH Follicle-stimulating hormone; stimulates eggs to mature and the production of oestrogen. Page 4

gametes Specialised sex cells involved in sexual reproduction in plants and animals. Page 11

gamma rays Part of the electromagnetic spectrum of waves that have the shortest wavelength. Page 50

generator A device that produces electricity when it spins. Power stations contain generators. Page 46

genes Parts of a chromosome that control an inherited characteristic. Page 11

genetic modification The deliberate modification of the characteristics of an organism by manipulating its genetic material. Page 12

global dimming Sunlight reaching the Earth is weakened as a result of atmospheric pollution. Page 28

global warming The gradual increase in the overall temperature of the Earth's atmosphere caused by increasing levels of greenhouse gases such as carbon dioxide and methane. Page 16

GM crops Genetically modified crops. These are crop plants that have had new genes added from another species. Page 12

greenhouse gases Gases such as carbon dioxide that help to trap heat energy in the atmosphere. Page 15

half-life The average time taken for half the atoms in a sample of a radioactive substance to decay. Page 52

herbicides Chemicals used to kill weeds. Page 14

hormones Chemicals that are transported around the body in the blood. These chemicals control body processes. Page 3

hydrocarbons Compounds made of carbon and hydrogen atoms only. Page 26

hydroelectric Using water flowing down a hill to make electricity. Page 46

hydrogels Strong gels that can be used to make contact lenses. Page 31

hydrogenation A chemical reaction where a hydrogen molecule joins with another compound, e.g. the hydrogenation of unsaturated oil to make saturated fat. Page 33

immune Protected against disease by the production of antibodies. Page 9

immunised Given a vaccine, containing dead or inactive pathogen, which stimulates the immune system to produce antibodies and memory cells. Page 9

impulses Form in which information is transmitted by nerve cells. Page 2

infra red A type of electromagnetic radiation that transfers thermal energy. Page 49

infra red radiation   Energy spreading out from a hot object in the form of waves. Page 41

ingesting   Taking food into the body. Page 8

inherited   Characteristic transmitted from parents to children via gametes (eggs and sperm). Page 5

insulators   Substances that are poor at conducting thermal energy. Page 40

ionisation   An ionised atom or molecule is electrically charged because it has lost or gained electrons. Page 53

ions   Charged particles. Page 53

isotopes   Atoms of an element come in different forms, depending on the numbers of neutrons they have in their nuclei. Page 52

LH   Luteinising hormone, which stimulates egg release. Page 4

lipoprotein   Proteins that are combined with fats or other lipids. Page 5

mantle   The middle, soft, rocky layer of the Earth that can move very slowly. Page 37

menstrual cycle   The monthly cycle of changes in a woman's reproductive system, controlled by hormones. Page 4

metabolic rate   A measure of the energy used by an animal in a given time period. Page 4

microwaves   Part of the electromagnetic spectrum of waves that have wavelengths from about 10 cm to 0.1 mm. Page 49

monomers   Small molecules that are joined up to form a polymer. Page 30

mortar   A paste made from slaked lime and water that was once used to stick bricks together. Page 21

National Grid   The system of power stations, cables and transformers that transfer electricity all over the country. Page 44

natural selection   The death of poorly adapted individuals and the survival of well-adapted individuals. Page 13

nerves   Bundles of neurones. Page 2

neurones   Cells specialised to transmit electrical nerve impulses and so carry information from one part of the body to another. Page 2

neutrons   Sub-atomic particles with no electric charge and a relative mass of 1. Page 52

noble gases   Gases from Group 0 of the Periodic table, e.g. helium, argon, neon. Page 39

non-renewable   Resources that, once used, cannot be replaced. Page 46

nucleus   The central part of the atom containing the proton(s) and, for all except hydrogen, the neutrons; has most of the mass of the atom. Page 18

ores   Natural compounds of a metal from which the metal can be extracted. Page 22

pathogens   Microorganisms that cause disease in plants or animals. Page 7

penicillin   Antibiotic produced by the mould *Penicillium*. Page 9

pesticides   Chemicals that kill pests such as insects. Page 14

polymers   Very long-chained molecules made by joining lots of small molecules together. Page 30

power   The rate at which energy is transformed. Page 45

power stations   Factories for producing electricity. Page 44

protons   Sub-atomic particles with a positive charge and a relative mass of 1. Page 52

quicklime   Calcium oxide (CaO), a strong base formed by heating limestone. Page 20

radiation   Energy spreading out from a source (e.g. infra red or light energy), or carried by particles (e.g. from a radioactive substance). Page 40

radio waves   Part of the electromagnetic spectrum of waves that have the longest wavelength. Page 49

radioactive   A radioactive material contains some atoms whose nuclei are unstable, and may spontaneously break down giving out radiation. Page 52

radioactive decay   When a radioactive atom decays, it emits radiation and becomes a different type of atom. Page 52

receptors   Organs or cells that are sensitive to external stimuli. Page 2

recycle   To re-use materials over and over again. Page 17

red-shift   The change in wavelength of light from a distant star; it looks redder because it is receding. Page 57

reduction   The removal of oxygen from a compound, e.g. iron oxide is reduced to iron. Page 23

reflection   When waves bounce off a surface. Page 49

reflex action   Rapid involuntary response to a particular stimulus. Page 2

Glossary and index

reliability The proportion of the time that a device is working. Some types of power station have greater reliability than others because they can work more of the time. Page 46

renewable An energy source that will not run out. Page 46.

resistance Ability to not be destroyed by the action of antibiotics. Page 5

saturated A carbon-chain molecule that only has single bonds between the carbon atoms. Page 26

sexual reproduction Biological process of reproduction involving the combination of genetic material from two parents. Page 11

slaked lime Calcium hydroxide ($Ca(OH)_2$), made by adding water to quicklime. Page 20

solar electric cell A device that converts light directly into electricity. Page 46

spectrum A series of waves, arranged in order according to their wavelengths and frequencies. Page 48

sperm The male sex cell (gamete). Page 11

statins Drugs that act to reduce levels of cholesterol in the blood. Page 6

step-down transformer A device that changes a high voltage into a lower one. Page 45

step-up transformer A device that changes a low voltage into a higher one. Page 45

stimulus A detectable change. Page 2

sustainable development Development that conserves natural resources. Page 17

synapse The junction between two nerve cells. Page 3

tectonic plates Massive sections of the Earth's crust that gradually move around the Earth's surface, transporting the continents. Page 37

temperature difference The difference in temperature between one object and another. Page 42

Thalidomide Drug formerly used as a sedative, but found to cause abnormalities in the developing fetus. Page 6

thermal decomposition Breaking down a chemical compound by heating. Page 20

thermal energy A form of energy; heat. The hotter an object, the more thermal energy it has. Page 40

tissue culture A cloning technique that involves growing groups of cells into new plants. Page 11

tracer A radioactive isotope that is used in medicine to follow the course of a biological process (e.g. digestion), providing information about the events in the process. Page 54

transfer Movement of energy from place to place. Page 40

transform To change energy from one form to another. Page 40

transformers Devices that change the voltage of an electricity supply. Page 45

transition metals The 'everyday' metals such as iron and copper, found in the central block of the periodic table. Page 25

transmission When waves are able to pass through a material. Page 49

turbine A device that is designed to turn in order to spin a generator. Page 46

ultra violet Part of the electromagnetic spectrum of waves that have wavelengths that are just shorter than those of visible light. Page 49

unsaturated A carbon-chain molecule that has at least one double bond between its carbon atoms. Page 29

useful energy The energy output from a device that is in the form we want. Page 42

vaccine Preparation made from dead or inactive pathogens, which can be injected so that the body makes antibodies to destroy live pathogens of that type. Page 9

viruses Types of microbes that cause disease; examples of such diseases are measles and the common cold. Page 7

visible light A very narrow band in the middle of the electromagnetic spectrum that enables us to see. Page 48

wasted energy The energy output from a device that is in a form we do not want. Page 42

wavelength The length of a single wave, measured from one wave crest to the next. Page 48

white blood cells Blood cells that counteract infection. Page 8

withdrawal symptoms Symptoms in a drug-dependent person who stops taking the drug or reduces the dosage. Page 7

X-rays Part of the electromagnetic spectrum of waves that have very short wavelengths, similar to the diameter of atoms. Page 50